Food Pets Die For

Shocking Facts About Pet Food

ANN N. MARTIN

Foreword by
Shawn Messonnier, DVM

NEWSAGE PRESS
TROUTDALE, OREGON

FOOD PETS DIE FOR:
Shocking Facts About Pet Food
Copyright 2003 © Ann N. Martin
New and Revised Edition, Paperback Original ISBN 0-939165-46-5
(First edition ISBN 0-939165-31-7)

NewSage Press
PO Box 607
Troutdale, OR 97060-0607
503-695-2211

website: www.newsagepress.com
email: info@newsagepress.com

Cover Design by George Foster
Book Design by Patricia Keelin, Production by Sherry Wachter
Printed in the United States on recycled paper with soy ink.

Distributed in the United States and Canada by
Publishers Group West 800-788-3123

*Note to the reader: This book is an informational guide. If you have questions
regarding the health of your animal companion and a possible problem related
to diet, consult a professional veterinarian, preferably one who is knowledgeable
in nutrition.*

Library of Congress Control Number: 2003389146

2 3 4 5 6 7 8 9 10

ACKNOWLEDGMENTS

This book is dedicated to Chuck.

No book like this can reach fruition without the help and input of many individuals. First and foremost my publisher and editor, Maureen Michelson who spent untold hours questioning, checking facts and pulling the material together to make a rough manuscript a readable book. My sincere thank you Maureen.

A special thank you to Tracy Smith for her proofreading and attention to detail. Also, thank you to the talented designers who made this book attractive and visually inviting: George Foster for the cover, and Sherry Wachter for the content design.

Shawn Messonnier, DVM, Michael Fox, DVM, Alfred Plechner, DVM, and Martin Zucker, I thank you so very much for your endorsements. You are all people I admire. I am humbled by your kind words.

To the many other veterinarians and specialists in various fields with whom I have corresponded, you have added immeasurable information, which has provided insight into the various topics covered. Although I can't thank you individually please know that you have played a very important role.

Chuck, my partner, my friend, thank you, from the bottom of my heart, for being there. Jamie, my son, without your computer knowledge my manuscript would have been lost numerous times. Thank you also for your persistence in attempting to capture some good photos of Sarge and the cats.

To my sister, Mary, my extended family, Irene, Darlene, Tina, Audrey, Sheila and their families, please know that you are all a very important part of my life. My friends, worldwide, who have provided so much information, please know that without your input many questions would have been left unanswered.

Last, but not least, my four-legged family: Sarge, our beautiful German shepherd and our felines—Ben, Simon, and Jake. You have been my taste testers for many, many years and survived to reach old age. I love you all.

A SPECIAL ENDORSEMENT

Every veterinarian should provide copies of this book for their clients, and everyone with a companion dog or cat should not be without it. Good nutrition is a cornerstone for health and disease prevention. Ann Martin documents how this cornerstone has been removed by the commercial pet food industry. They recycle and profit from the by-products of the human food industry, including the diseased and condemned parts of cruelly raised, factory-farmed animals. This practice puts millions of dogs, cats, and other animals as well as humans at risk.

Food Pets Die For is part of the ongoing revolution in agriculture and the food industry that calls on informed consumers to support a more humane, organic, sustainable, and healthful food production system.

I am honored to again endorse this book in its second edition because Ann Martin's investigative writing has helped set the record straight on a multi-billion dollar pet food industry. With this information we can all act responsibly by making informed choices for the health and well being of our beloved animal companions.

—MICHAEL W. FOX
Veterinarian, Bioethicist, and Author

CONTENTS

Foreword

Ann Martin presents information that is informative, eye-opening, and groundbreaking in exposing the truth behind what is contained in many commercially produced pet foods. While the information contained in *Food Pets Die For* may appear controversial and will likely be dismissed by some, it is well-researched information.

She points out the dangers that are often present in many brands of commercial pet food and encourages you to learn more about just what is contained in that bag or can before you feed it to your pet. In short, Ann Martin presents an answer that at times is not too pleasant to the all-important question I pose, *Do you really know what your pet ate last night?*

As a practicing holistic veterinarian, I am constantly amazed that diet is often the most neglected part of a pet's health care. It's not that most pet owners don't want to feed their pets properly, it's just that they think they are doing so simply because they have purchased one of the "recommended premium foods" advertised or promoted by the pet store clerk or even by their own veterinarians.

I used to believe that simply recommending a premium food was enough. Somehow my limited knowledge of nutrition qualified me to believe that following the advice of a pet food company and then making that food available to my clients ensured they would feed a healthy diet. When I decided to change my focus of treating disease to healing pets and began incorporating a holistic approach at my practice, I realized that the only thing "premium" about the diets I had recommended was the price!

By learning all I could about pet nutrition and the pet food industry, I have changed my recommendation. Now I know better. As Ann Martin discusses here the best diet is a homemade one, using the freshest, most wholesome ingredients. Next best is a diet from a company that truly uses wholesome protein, fat, and carbohydrate sources in the diet, without relying on toxic chemicals and preservatives. Either choice of diet can be made even better with proper nutritional supplementation.

In my pre-veterinary studies I was an animal science major. One of my favorite classes was meat science, where I learned how to properly process meat for the consumer. I was quite impressed that literally nothing from the slaughtered animal carcass was ever wasted. What wasn't wholesome for human consumption was sold to the pet food industry.

At the time, I appreciated that there was no waste in the processing plant. Now that I have learned more about pet nutrition, I'm not quite so impressed. The waste that ends up in our pets' food would be better used as fertilizer. The reason many companies rely on slaughterhouse waste for raw pet food ingredients is cost: it is simply cheaper to use the trash from the slaughterhouse than whole fresh meats and organs. No thought is given to what feeding waste products might do to a pet's health.

As a practicing veterinarian, I can honestly say that most of my clients would gladly spend a few extra dollars for their pets' food if it was made of quality ingredients and contributed to (rather than detracted from) their pets' health. No longer can we make cost an issue. As Ann Martin clearly explains, "If it had not been for the illness of my two dogs in 1990 I would likely still be feeding commercial pet foods, thinking I was doing what is best for my beloved pets. I would also still be paying vet bills almost on a monthly basis."

Yes, it's true: taking a holistic approach to pet care does usually save the pet owner money on veterinary bills. Starting with a wholesome diet is the first concern that should be addressed in any holistic pet care program.

If more people knew what is contained in many processed foods and complained to the manufacturers, my guess is that we would see more wholesome diets produced. One of my personal goals is to work with any of the "big name" pet food companies to create a holistic diet they can be proud of and owners can confidently feed to their pets. Use the information in this book and learn to feed your pet the best food possible. Good luck on your road to better pet health!

—SHAWN MESSONNIER, DVM
The Natural Health Bible for Dogs & Cats
Paws & Claws Animal Hospital, Plano, Texas

INTRODUCTION

There is information in this book that may not be easy to accept, but if you care about your animal companions, and you want to be informed about what is in most commercial pet foods, then keep reading. I have carefully documented my sources throughout the book because I know some will question if it is really possible that so many disgusting ingredients can be legally added to commercial pet food. I have taken great care to responsibly make my case about the dangers of most commercial pet foods. I have also included in this new edition suggestions on healthy pet foods, and better yet, included more recipes for homemade meals for your companion animals.

Since writing the original edition of *Food Pets Die For* in 1997 and exposing what goes into those attractive cans and bags of commercial pet food, a growing number of consumers are realizing that many of the claims made by commercial pet food companies about their products being "balanced and nutritional" are false.

While researching and writing, there were times that I was absolutely horrified with what I discovered. There were other times when I was extremely frustrated with the run-around I received from government agencies, organizations involved with the pet food industry, the rendering industry, and at times, veterinary research centers. What has kept me going is the hope that pet owners will read my findings and be convinced that their pets' health is directly related to what they eat—and that most commercial pet foods are garbage.

In 1990 after the illness of my two large dogs, Louie, a Saint Bernard, and Charlie, a Newfoundland, I began to ask questions about the ingredients in commercial pet foods and the manufacturers. I quickly learned that this is a multi-billion dollar industry that operates with virtually no government regulations and in many ways is self-regulated. I also learned that there are many deplorable ingredients that legally can be used in pet foods as sources of protein—in particular, euthanized cats and dogs, diseased cattle and horses, roadkill, dead zoo animals, and meat not fit for human consumption. In addition, sources of fiber in many foods are composed of the leftovers from the food chain, including beet pulp, the residue of sugar beets, peanut hulls, and even sawdust sweepings from the floor of the rendering plant!

The latest information in this new edition reflects several years of persistent questioning and research. I have gone back, numerous times, to government agencies in order to obtain the information I requested. In some situations I had to use the Freedom of Information Act.

When you are dealing with a multi-billion dollar industry that wants to continue in the same mode, using the same dubious ingredients, and condoning inhumane research on animals, change will only come in small increments. This is a battle that will continue. Getting answers may take time. Getting changes, and perhaps regulations, will take even more time—but it is something that anyone who cares about their pets must question and hopefully, demand reform.

If it had not been for the illness of my two dogs in 1990 I would likely still be feeding commercial pet foods, thinking I was doing what is best for my beloved pets. I would also still be paying vet bills almost on a monthly basis. And ultimately, I would not have been aware that my pets who have died over the years were ending up at a rendering plant.

I always hold out the hope that in writing these books and in sharing the information I have acquired over many years, pet owners will give their animal companions better nutrition. I also hope that when cats and dogs die, their bodies will not end up in a rendering vat, but rather be cremated or buried in a dignified and respectful manner. This is the least we can do for our animal companions.

—Ann N. Martin
November 2002

– ONE –

What Goes into Commercial Pet Food

Television commercials and magazine advertisements for pet food would have us believe that the meats, grains, and fats used could grace our own dining tables. Choice chicken, beef, lamb, whole grains, and quality fats are supposedly the composition of commercially produced dog and cat food.

In recent years some small pet food companies have begun to use human grade ingredients in their products to provide healthy and nutritious food. However, the standard fare from most commercial pet food companies is far from nutritious. In fact many of the ingredients are potentially harmful and composed of the dregs from slaughterhouses and the rendering business. Even some of the "premium foods" promoted by pet food companies are really not any different than their standard line—other than being more expensive.

So, how do you determine if a particular pet food is nutritious or not? Ultimately, the best defense is to feed your animal companions human grade food, either homecooked, or made by pet food companies that use human grade foods. If you decide to feed your animal companions commercial pet foods that do not use human grade ingredients, then read the labels. And even then, *buyer beware.*

Deciphering Pet Food Labels

Pet food labels can be deceiving—they only provide half the story. The other half of the story is hidden behind obscure ingredients listed on the label. Even conscientious consumers couldn't possibly detect the hidden ingredients that can be legally put in pet food, because only about half the actual contents of the pet food are listed on the label due to minimal legal regulations. In addition it is not easy to understand what the list of ingredients truly implies. The only way that I have figured this out is by unearthing the information slowly, bit by bit.

For instance, it took me awhile to discern what it means when certain words are listed, such as "meat by-product." The word "meat" sounds good and implies protein, but I have learned that "meat by-product" can include a variety of unsavory animal parts. According to Association of American Feed Control Officials (AAFCO), "Meat by-product is the nonrendered, clean parts of slaughtered mammals other than the meat."

Under AAFCO guidelines, acceptable meat by-product can include animal lungs, spleens, kidneys, brains, livers, blood, bones, low-temperature fatty tissue, and stomachs and intestines freed of their contents. Livers can be infested with worms (liver flukes) or diseased with cirrhosis. Lungs can be filled with pneumonia. If an animal is diseased and declared unfit for human consumption, the carcass is acceptable for pet food. Even parts of animals, such as "stick marks,"—the area of the body where animals have been injected with antibiotics, hormones, or other drugs—are cut from the carcasses intended for human consumption and used for meat by-product for pet food.

The most objectionable source of protein for pet food is euthanized cats and dogs. *(See Chapter Two.)* It is not uncommon for thousands of euthanized dogs and cats to be delivered to rendering plants, daily, and thrown into the rendering vat—collars, I.D. tags, and plastic bags—to become part of this material called "meat meal."

I have listed some of the ingredients frequently included on pet food labels. These definitions are from AAFCO's "Ingredient Definitions." It is important to note that when you read descriptions that include "clean flesh" or "clean parts" that this concept is ambiguous. In an article written by David C. Cooke," Animal Disposal: Fact and Fiction," Cooke asks, "Can you imagine trying to remove the hair and stomach contents from 600,000 tons of dogs and cats prior to cooking them? It would seem that either the Association of American Feed Control Officials' [AAFCO] definition of meat meal or meat and bone meal should be redefined or it needs to include a better description of good factory practices."[1]

Meat, Poultry, and Fish Sources

Meat: AAFCO defines "meat" as the clean flesh derived from slaughtered mammals. This mammal flesh is limited to the part of the striate muscle that is skeletal or what is found in the tongue, diaphragm, heart, or esophagus. AAFCO stipulates that the flesh is "with or without the accompanying and overlying fat and the portions of the skin, sinew, nerve, and blood vessels that normally accompany the flesh." When you read on a pet food label that the product contains "real meat," you are getting blood vessels, sinew, and so on. Meat is not rendered but comes directly from slaughterhouses.

Meat meal: AAFCO defines "meat meal" as the rendered product from mammal tissue exclusive of blood, hair, hoof, hide, trimmings, manure, stomach, and rumen contents except in such amounts as may occur unavoidably in good processing practices. (The rumen is the first stomach, also called the cud, of a cud-chewing animal.)

Poultry-by-product meal: This consists of ground, rendered, clean parts of slaughtered poultry, including necks, feet, undeveloped eggs, and intestines, exclusive of feathers, except in such amounts as might occur unavoidably in good processing practices.

Poultry-hatchery by-product: This ingredient can include a mixture of eggshells, infertile and unhatched eggs, and culled chicks that have been cooked, dried, and ground, with or without removal of part of the fat.

Poultry by-product: This can include nonrendered clean parts of slaughtered poultry such as heads, feet, and viscera, free of fecal content and foreign matter except in such trace amounts as might occur unavoidably in good factory practice.

Hydrolyzed poultry feather: AAFCO considers this another source of protein—not digestible protein, but protein nonetheless. This product results from a pressure treatment of clean, intact feathers from slaughtered poultry, free of additives, and/or accelerators. (An accelerator makes the feathers compost faster.)

Fish: If you live with a cat, just open a can of food that contains fish and watch kitty come running. The parts used are fish heads, tails, fins, bones, and viscera. If the label lists "fish," this means that the fish parts come directly from the fish processing plants and do not go through the rendering process.

R.L. Wysong, DVM, states that because the entire fish is not used for most commercial pet foods, it does not contain many of the fat soluble vitamins, minerals, and omega-3 fatty acids necessary for good nutrition. When the entire fish is used for commercial pet food, oftentimes it is because the fish contains a high level of mercury or other toxin making it unfit for human consumption. Tuna is used in many cat foods because of its strong odor, which many cats find irresistible.

Fish meal: This product is created by rendering residue from the fish processing plants and might include heads, tails, innards, and blood. Fish meal is generally higher in protein quality then meat and bone meal. AAFCO defines fish meal as "clean, dried, ground tissue of undecomposed whole fish or fish cuttings, either or both, with or without the extraction of part of the oil."

Other Protein Sources

According to AAFCO, there are a number of other sources that can make up the protein in pet foods. If you have a weak stomach, proceed at your own risk.

Hydrolyzed hair is made from clean hair treated by heat and pressure to produce a product suitable for animal feeding. This includes the hair from cattle, horses, pigs, or other animals who have been slaughtered.

Spray-dried animal blood is produced from clean, fresh animal blood, exclusive of all extraneous material such as hair, stomach belching (contents of stomach), and urine, except in such traces as might occur unavoidably in good factory practices. Blood from these animals can be used in pet food, either mixed with other materials in the rendering process, or formed into the meat chunks that are found in some canned foods.

Dehydrated food-waste is any and all animal and vegetable produce picked up from basic food processing sources or institutions, including garbage from hospitals, restaurants, and grocery stores. The produce has to be picked up daily or sufficiently often so that no decomposition is evident. With this ingredient, it seems that what you don't see won't hurt you.

Dehydrated garbage is composed of artificially dried animal and vegetable waste collected frequently so that harmful decomposition has not set in. AAFCO stipulates that dehydrated garbage should be separated from crockery, glass, metal, string, and similar materials. This might include waste from butcher shops or processing plants that process fruits and vegetables.

Dehydrated paunch products (ingested food and water) are composed of the contents of the rumen of slaughtered cattle, dehydrated at temperatures over 212° F. (100° C.) to a moisture content of 12 percent or less. Such dehydration is designed to destroy any pathogenic bacteria.

Dried poultry waste is an animal waste product composed primarily of processed ruminant excreta that has been artificially dehydrated to a moisture content not in excess of 15 percent. According to AAFCO, "It shall contain not less than 12 percent crude protein, not more than 40 percent crude fiber, including straw, wood shavings, and so on, and not more than 30 percent ash." This material is often obtained from factory farming operations.

Dried swine waste is an animal waste product composed primarily of swine excreta that has been artificially dehydrated to a moisture content not in excess of 15 percent. AAFCO states that "it shall contain not less than 20 percent crude protein, not more than 35 percent crude fiber, including other material such as straw, wood shavings, or acceptable bedding materials, and not more than 20 percent ash." As with the poultry waste, this often comes from large hog operations.

Undried processed animal waste product is composed of excreta, with or without the litter (litter is the ground covering in the chicken pens) from poultry, ruminants, or any other animal except humans. This may or may not include other feed ingredients, and contains more than 15 percent feed ingredients, and more than 15 percent moisture. AAFCO stipulates that this product "shall contain no more than 30 percent combined wood, wood shavings, litter, dirt, sand, rocks, and similar extraneous materials."

Grain Sources

In addition to the sources of proteins that can be used in these foods, AAFCO also has an extensive list of various grains that can be used in pet foods, horse feed, and cattle feed.

Corn: This is the main ingredient in dry food for dogs and cats. According to AAFCO, there is a long list of corn products that can be used in pet food. These include, but are not limited to, the following ingredients.

Corn flour: This is the fine-size, hard flinty portion of ground corn containing little or none of the bran or germ.

Corn bran: This is the outer coating of the corn kernel, with little or none of the starchy part of the germ.

Corn gluten meal: This is the dried residue from corn after the removal of the larger part of the starch and germ, and the separation of the bran by the process employed in the wet milling manufacture of corn starch or syrup, or by enzymatic treatment of the endosperm.

Wheat: This ingredient is found in many pet foods, and again, AAFCO gives several terms for wheat products.

Wheat flour: This consists principally of wheat flour together with fine particles of wheat bran, wheat germ, and the offal from the "tail of the mill." Tail of the mill is nothing more then the sweepings of leftovers after everything has been processed from the wheat.

Wheat germ meal: This consists chiefly of wheat germ together with some bran and middlings or shorts.

Wheat middlings and shorts: These are also categorized as the fine particles of wheat germ, bran, flour, and offal from the "tail of the mill."

"Splitting" in Labeling

Corn and wheat are usually the first ingredients listed on both dry dog and cat food labels. However, some pet food companies list the product ingredients in such a way that the number one ingredient is a protein product. In one well-known dry cat food the ingredients on the label are listed in this order: poultry by-product meal, ground yellow corn, wheat, corn gluten meal, soybean meal, brewers rice, etc.

Most people reading this label might assume that the "poultry by-product meal" is the prime ingredient providing an ample source of protein. However, this is not so. Grains in fact are the prime ingredients in the product. In the industry this labeling is called "splitting." If corn is listed in only one form, then it might be the prime ingredient in the food instead of the poultry meal and would have to be listed first on the label. To make it appear that a protein source is the number one ingredient in the pet food, the company splits the corn up into two categories; ground yellow corn and corn gluten meal.

This can be problematic for consumers who believe a dry food is sufficient for their animal companions, especially cats. Cats are carnivores and require a good source of meat in their diets. So pet owners who think it's okay to just feed their cats a dry food are not providing a healthy diet. Grains will not provide the cat with sufficient amounts of taurine, arachidonic acid, vitamin A or vitamin B-12.

Toxic Substances in Grain

The contamination of grains used in pet food, particularly mycotoxins, can be deadly. Mycotoxins are toxic substances produced by fungi in moldy grains and they are found in rye, corn, barley, oats, wheat, peanuts, Brazil nuts, pecans, and walnuts. More than three hundred types of mycotoxins exist worldwide.

The most common mycotoxins, aflatoxins B1, are known carcinogens in laboratory animals and presumably in our pets. Fumonisin B1 and B2 are molds that are common natural contaminants of corn. Recent animal studies have indicated that the B1 variety of this toxin is also carcinogenic.

Ochratoxin A, found mainly in cereal grains, corn, barley, wheat, and oats, is another carcinogen. Ochratoxin A is not completely destroyed in processing and cooking food.

Deoxynivalenol (DON) also known as vomitoxin, is a common contaminate of wheat, barley, rye, and corn. Pets who eat grains contaminated with vomitoxin can have symptoms that include refusal to eat, vomiting, and diarrhea.

In 1995, Nature's Recipe recalled $20 million worth of its dog food because inspectors found vomitoxin in "wheat screenings" used in the pet food. (Wheat screenings, which are not used for human consumption, can include broken grains, crop and weed seeds, hulls, chaff, joints, straw, elevator or mill dust, sand, and dirt.) The FDA did investigate but not out of concern for the more than 250 dogs who became ill after eating Nature's Recipe. The FDA investigated because of concerns for human health. The contaminated wheat screenings included the end product of wheat flour that was used for making pasta for human consumption. (Wheat for baking flour requires a higher quality of wheat.)

In another case of mycotoxin poisoning, aflatoxin caused the death of at least twenty-five dogs in 1998. Doane Products Company, a Tennessee company that produces dry and semi-moist foods as well as soft treats and dog biscuits for numerous pet food companies, had produced the contaminated pet food. The recall included at least fifty brands, including Ol'Roy, Winchester, and Hill Country Fare, all of which were suspected of being contaminated with aflatoxin.

Many of the grains used in commercial pet food contain levels of herbicides, pesticides, and fungicides that are cancer-causing agents. These are grains that did not pass inspection for use in human foods because of the levels of herbicides, pesticides, fungicides, or mycotoxins; however, they are deemed fit for use in pet foods. Little, if any, testing or research is undertaken to determine levels of these toxic substances in pet foods.

Additional Pet Food Ingredients

In addition to the main sources of ingredients used in commercial pet foods there are other ingredients that can be added, according to AAFCO.

Beet pulp: The dried residue from sugar beet, added for fiber, but primarily sugar.

Soybean meal: Obtained by grinding the flakes that remain after the removal of most of the oil from soybeans by a solvent extraction process.

Powdered cellulose: This ingredient is purified, mechanically disintegrated cellulose. It is a white, odorless, tasteless product prepared by processing alpha cellulose obtained as a pulp from fibrous plant material. Powdered cellulose is used as a bulking agent in pet foods.

Sugar foods by-products: This ingredient is created by grinding and mixing inedible portions derived from the preparation and packaging of sugar-based food products such as candy, dry-packaged drinks, dried gelatin mixes, and similar food products that are largely composed of sugar.

Ground almond and peanut shells: Another source of fiber.

Vitamins and Minerals in Pet Food

On the labels of dog and cat food you will notice an extensive list of substances, many of which are vitamins and minerals. Some of the vitamins added to pet foods:

- **Choline Chloride:** member of the B complex
- **Calcium Panthenate:** vitamin B-5
- **Thiamin Mononitrate:** vitamin B-1
- **Riboflavin Supplement:** vitamin B-2
- **Pyridoxine Hydrochloride:** vitamin B-6
- **Folic Acid:** vitamin B-9
- **Biotin Supplement:** vitamin K
- **Menadione Dimethylprimidinol Bisulfite:** source of vitamin K
- **Ascorbic Acid:** vitamin C

The prime minerals that are added to pet food include zinc, iron, and copper. These minerals can, in some cases, cause serious health problems for pets, particularly if you happen to get a bag of food that has an inordinate amount of minerals added. This was how my dogs initially got sick in 1990. I had the dry dog food tested at an independent lab, and the test results showed a zinc level twenty times higher than the daily recommended dose. Veterinarians versed in toxicology whom I contacted explained that zinc levels in excess of 1,000 parts per million (ppm) can be toxic for dogs. The Recommended Daily Allowance (RDA) for dogs is approximately 50 mg. per day.

Other minerals often listed on a pet food label:

Iron proteinate, ferrous carbonate, and ferrous sulfate: These are necessary for the production of hemoglobin. Deficiencies will manifest themselves as anemia and fatigue. Natural sources of iron include liver, kidney, lean meats, shellfish, fruits, nuts, whole grains, leafy vegetables and blackstrap molasses. Ferrous sulfate can deplete vitamin E, which many "natural" pet foods use as a preservative.[2]

Copper oxide and copper proteinate: These are necessary for converting the iron into hemoglobin. The liver stores the excess copper that the body is unable to use. Excess copper can result in liver disease. For example, Bedlington terriers can inherit hemolytic anemia, characterized by an abnormal accumulation of copper in the liver.

Copper sulfate: This is a cheap copper supplement that the pet food industry chose to add to the pet foods. It is in many pet foods, however it may pose a major threat to your pet's health. Copper has been described in a toxicology research paper undertaken by four universities as "highly corrosive to plain steel, iron, and galvanized pipes."[3] People handling this material have been advised to wear boots, protective gloves, and goggles, yet this material may be added to both livestock and pet food.

Copper sulfate is stored in the liver, brain, heart, kidneys, and muscles of livestock who ingest it through the feed. Copper is stable in heat, cold, and light although there is slight decomposition at temperatures about 392° F. (200° C.) However, in the rendering process temperatures usually do not exceed 270 ° F. (132.2° C.), so it is highly likely that the copper sulfate in slaughtered cattle will be intact when rendered into pet food. This means that in addition to pet food companies adding the copper supplement, the mineral could also be present in meat by-product for pet food due to rendered cattle.

Preservatives in Pet Foods

Take note that commercial pet food companies usually purchase large quantities of these vitamins and minerals already mixed together, called premixes. This means that your pet is ingesting preservatives from a number of different sources. Artificial flavors, garlic, cheese, and bacon are often added to pet foods to make it more palatable. These flavors, plus the added dyes, which turn the gray matter a bright red, are to give the consumer the impression that the can of dog or cat food is wholesome.

BHA and BHT are two preservatives that have long been suspected as being carcinogenic. Both are chemical antioxidants that prevent the fatty contents of pet food from becoming rancid. The foods have an endless shelf life with these preservatives,

In a letter to the Center for Veterinary Medicine, Wendell Belfield, DVM, addressed the dubious ingredients in pet foods. He wrote, "Chemicals such as BHA, BHT which can initiate birth defects, and damage to liver and kidneys are commonly used preservatives."[4] These preservatives are also found in the human food chain, however, you must remember that we are not ingesting them at every meal as our companion animals may well be if they are eating the same processed pet food daily.

Ethoxyquin is another antioxidant preservative that has since been proven to be highly toxic to animals. It was developed by Monsanto and used extensively in pet foods, however, due to protests from many pet owners, ethoxyquin is not as prevalent as it once was. Yet, it is still approved by the Food and Drug Administration, Center for Veterinary Medicine, as a preservative in pet food.

The Animal Protection Institute (API), stated in a 1996 report: "Ethoxyquin has been associated with immune deficiency syndrome, leukemia, blindness, skin, stomach, spleen and liver cancer in companion animals."[5] Many pet food companies state that they do not add this substance to their foods. What they neglect to mention is that their suppliers, the suppliers of the raw material used in pet foods—the meat and fats—can add ethoxyquin before they ship it to the pet food company. The pet food company does not need to state this on the label. Pet food companies simply have to state what they have added, not what their suppliers have added to the raw material. If you ever see this preservative listed on a can or bag of food, *stay away from that product.*

Fats in Pet Food

Fats can be sprayed directly on pet food or mixed with the other ingredients. Fats give off a pungent odor that entices your pet to eat the garbage. These fats are sourced from restaurant grease, which is often rancid and certainly unfit for human consumption. Another main source of fat comes from the rendering plant. This is obtained from the tissues of mammals and/or poultry in the commercial rendering process described in the next section.

The Rendering Process

Before I began learning about what goes into commercial pet foods, I knew nothing about rendering plants or how product for pet food was manufactured. Rendering facilities have been around for hundreds of years, yet the general public knows very little about this industry. And I am sure that most people do not know that a lot of the by-product created by rendering plants ends up in commercial pet food.

Renderers accept the waste and leftovers from our society. This includes animals picked up by dead stock removal companies; dead zoo animals; roadkill too large to be buried at the side of the road; restaurant and grocery store garbage, including the styrofoam trays and plastic wrap; and hundreds of thousands of euthanized cats and dogs.

Slaughterhouses also provide renderers with the leftovers from slaughtered animals not fit for human consumption. Before these animal parts and by-product used for pet food are shipped from the slaughterhouse to the rendering plant, the by-product is "denatured." This means that crude carbolic acid, cresylic disinfectant, or citronella, is sprayed on the product. In the case of a whole beef or swine carcass that has been condemned, the denaturing product is injected into the entire carcass. If meat inspectors condemn only parts of an animal, the United States Department of Agriculture (USDA) requires that "before an approved denaturing agent is applied, the product must be freely slashed so that pieces are less than 4" in diameter. This allows the denaturant to contact all parts of the product."[6]

In Canada the denaturing agent is Birkolene B. When I asked the Ministry of Agriculture what was in Birkolene B, the representative would not divulge its composition, stating its ingredients are a "trade secret." Keep in mind that the substances used to denature are toxic. Cresylic acid, a tar-oil derivative, has replaced fuel oil as a denaturing substance. In the United States, the Occupational Safety and Health Administration (OSHA) classifies both crude carbolic acid and cresylic as "poison."

At the rendering plant a machine slowly grinds the entire mess in huge vats. Then this product is cooked at temperatures between 220° F. and 270° F. (104.4° C. to 132.2° C.) for twenty minutes to one hour. The mixture is centrifuged (spun at a high speed) and the grease (or tallow) rises to the top and it is removed from the mixture. The grease becomes the source of animal fat in most pet foods. Oftentimes, when you open a standard can of dog food, you will see a top layer of fat. The centrifuged product is the source of that fat, which is meant to entice a hungry dog or cat.

After the grease is removed in the rendering process, the remaining material is dried. Meat meal, and meat and bone meal are the end product of this process. This dried material is usually found in dry pet food.

Can This Really Be True?

After reading the list of ingredients from AAFCO for the first time and not really believing that such ingredients could be used in pet food, I sent a fax to the chair of AAFCO to inquire, "Would the 'Feed Ingredient Definitions' apply to pet food as well as livestock feed?" The reply was as follows: "The feed ingredient definitions approved by AAFCO apply to all animal feeds, including pet foods, unless specific animal species restrictions are noted."[7] AAFCO confirmed what I hoped was not true.

I also found it difficult to believe that rendering plants produced much of the by-product used by commercial pet food companies. This disbelief has resulted in years of questioning government organizations, pet food manufacturers, renderers, animal-welfare organizations, and veterinarians.

The pet food industry claims to care about the health and welfare of our pets by providing complete and balanced diets. It is apparent from the ingredients used in these foods that they are nutritionally devoid of healthy and wholesome ingredients. In my opinion, the vitamin and mineral supplements, which are added to make up for what is lacking in the foods, are also inferior. We simply cannot expect our animal companions to enjoy good health and a long life if we feed them a garbage diet.

– *Two* –

Companion Animals in Pet Food

As this new edition of *Food Pets Die For* goes to press in the winter of 2002, I still have *no* doubt that the carcasses of cats and dogs continue to be rendered into product used in many commercial pet foods. It is clear, not only by the research I have conducted, but also by recent independent media investigations that dog and cat carcasses are in many commercial pet foods.

Pet food companies deny that any of their products contain rendered companion animals. They claim to ask their suppliers not to include cats and dogs; however, I have yet to find a pet food company that actually tests the raw material that it receives from a rendering plant to ascertain the sources of the protein. I also have to challenge commercial pet food companies' claims based on the well-established fact that rendering plants are oftentimes located near pet food companies. In my book, *Protect Your Pet,* I laid out my findings directly linking rendering plants that pick up carcasses from veterinary clinics and shelters and transport them to the rendering plant located near the pet food companies.

Numerous times I have questioned the Pet Food Institute (PFI), the non-governmental organization that oversees the pet food industry in the United States, if the pet food companies it represents test the raw material. I have asked representatives if they are aware that rendered dogs and cats can be in the meat meal used in many products. PFI has not answered these specific questions.

In 1990 when I began investigating the ingredients used in commercial pet food, a veterinarian in the United States advised me that the use of pets in pet food was routine practice. Rendering is a cheap viable means of disposal for euthanized pets. Pets are mixed with other materials, including condemned material from slaughterhouse facilities, rotten meat from supermarket shelves, restaurant grease and garbage, "4-D" (dead, diseased, dying, and disabled) animals, roadkill, and zoo animals. As explained in Chapter One, these ingredients are listed as "meat meal" on pet food labels.

Disposing of Euthanized Cats and Dogs

Before 1990, I had never heard of rendering. When my pets died I usually had the veterinarian dispose of the pets' bodies because I lived in a condominium and I did not have a place to bury them. I always assumed that the veterinary clinic made sure the pets were either buried or cremated. When I asked the vet about the disposal of the body, I was told, "Don't worry, we'll take care of it."

Now, I know better—"taking care of it" could include disposal to a rendering plant. Since 1990 I have communicated with dozens of veterinarians in the United States and in Canada to find out what they know about the disposal of euthanized animal companions after the bodies are picked up, usually by dead stock removal companies. Only three veterinarians were aware that the animal carcasses could be going to rendering plants. The rest all assumed that the dead pets were cremated.

When I asked Alan Schulman, DVM, who works at a veterinary hospital in Los Angeles, about the disposal of euthanized pets, he stated, "In our hospital, the options for owners are to take the remains of their pet for burial at the L.A. pet cemetery, or we utilize CalPet Crematory for individual cremations of pets with return of the ashes in an urn to the pet owners."[1]

Some veterinarians, including Lynn Nelson in Santa Monica, California, stated that about 50 percent of pet owners want their pets cremated. For the owners who do not want cremation, a company picks up the dead pets once a week from the vet clinic and delivers them to a rendering plant.

The shelters I corresponded with had a little different perspective. Most were aware that the company they contracted with trucked the animals to rendering plants. Few vet clinics or shelters have their own cremation facility.

"Thousands and thousands of pounds of dogs and cats are picked up and brought here every day,"[2] an employee of Sacramento Rendering told John Eckhouse of *The San Francisco Chronicle.* In 1990 Eckhouse was among the first to report this rendering practice. One rendering-plant employee told Eckhouse that the company "rendered somewhere between 10,000 and 30,000 pounds of dogs and cats a day out of a total of 250,000 to 500,000 pounds of cattle, poultry, butcher shop scraps and other material." I am sure those figures have grown in the past decade.

When I asked an employee at the Escondido Humane Society in Southern California, Phil Morgan, what they did with euthanized animals, Morgan replied, "Currently the Escondido Humane Society has a company called D&D Disposal. They pick up eight barrels a week of approximately 100 plus bodies. My understanding is they are rendered in Vernon, California. San Diego County has three shelters that last year put down close to 20 thousand animals, and that does not include animals hit by cars and other reasons for deaths." Morgan added, "There are a dozen other shelters with numbers close to mine—give or take—in addition to over a hundred vets in San Diego producing ten to twenty animals a month for pickup."[3]

When I asked the California shelters and veterinary clinics if they could provide me with the names of the disposal companies picking up these animals most were willing to provide this information. Dead stock removal companies and disposal companies are basically the same, although the dead stock removal operations pick up more dead livestock than companion animals. Nearly all clinics and shelters named the same two companies: D&D Disposal, Inc. and Koefran, Inc. West Coast Rendering owns D&D Disposal and Reno Rendering owns Koefran, Inc.

Some veterinarians were aware that these stock removal companies were subsidiaries of rendering companies and that the rendering plant would be the final destination of these animals. Many veterinarians, especially from shelters, confided that the facility did not have the funds for burial or cremation, so stock removal was the logical choice.

Rendering Pets in the United States

The rendering of companion animals is legal in the United States. There are no laws determining how veterinarians or shelters must dispose of pets. It is up to the owner, veterinarian, or shelter. For large animals, such as cattle, horses, and pigs, there is the "Dead Animal Disposal Act," which states they must be disposed of within twenty-four to forty-eight hours, depending on the state, and either be buried, cremated, or sent to rendering. But no similar disposal act exists for companion animals.

In 1994 I contacted the Food and Drug Administration/Center for Veterinary Medicine (FDA/CVM) and posed this question: Are government agencies aware that euthanized pets are being used in commercial pet foods? The reply I received from Christine Richmond, spokesperson for the FDA, Division of Animal Feeds, reads in part, "In recognizing the need for disposal of a large number of unwanted pets in this country, CVM has not acted to specifically prohibit the rendering of pets. However, that is not to say that the practice of using this material in pet food is condoned by CVM."[4] Even though the FDA/CVM does not condone the use of euthanized pets in pet food, it has not taken any steps to eliminate or restrict this practice.

Nationwide, rendering plants claim that dogs and cats are just a small percentage of the material that they render and that they are providing a much-needed service to shelters that can't afford other means of disposal such as cremation or burial. In a 1997 article in *The New York Times,* reporter Sandra Blakeslee quotes Chuck Ellis, a spokesman for the city's sanitation department: "Los Angeles sends 200 tons of euthanized cats and dogs to West Coast Rendering in Los Angeles, every month."[5]

Doug Anderson, president of Darling International, a large rendering company in Dallas, Texas, maintains that pet food companies try not to buy meat and bone meal from renderers that grind up cats and dogs. "We do not accept companion animals," he said. "But there are still a number of small plants that will render anything."[6]

Basically, there are two types of rendering plants. Plants that operate in conjunction with animal slaughterhouses or poultry processing plants are called integrated rendering plants. Plants that collect their raw materials from a variety of offsite sources are called independent rendering plants. Independent plants obtain animal by-product materials, "including grease, blood, feathers, offal, and the entire animal carcasses, from the following sources: butcher shops, supermarkets, restaurants, fast-food chains, poultry processors, slaughterhouses, farms, ranches, feedlots, and animal shelters."[7] All of the large rendering plants, including Darling International, Sacramento Rendering, West Coast Rendering, Baker Commodities Inc., Modesto Tallow, Carolina By-Products, Griffin Industries Inc., Rothsay, and Valley Proteins are independent renderers.

Rendering Pets in Canada

In Canada, it is legal to use euthanized pets in pet food product produced by rendering plants. However, rendering of companion animals in Canada is on a much smaller scale than the practice in the United States. But nonetheless, the practice is legal in Canada too.

In Ontario, the province where I reside, a dead-stock removal collector picks up any dead livestock that have died or been killed in the field. Different municipalities also contract with a stock removal collector to pick up any large animals along the roadside as well as companion animals euthanized at veterinary clinics and some shelters. The collector then delivers the dead stock to a rendering plant.

The Canadian Ministry keeps records of the dead stock going through the system, but no records are kept on the number of companion animals, roadkill, or zoo animals processed. This also applies in the United States. The U.S. Department of

Agriculture does not require that records be kept of rendered dogs or cats.

In 1992, I asked the investigator from the Canadian ministry, "How are the dogs and cats disposed of that this company picks up?" Two months later I received a letter along with a document from the dead-stock removal company. The document was addressed to the Chief Investigator, David Sloman, who works for the Ministry of Agriculture and Food. It was also stamped "Confidential" and "not to be made known to any other agency or person without the written permission of the Chief Investigator."

It was clear why the dead-stock removal company did not want this information released. The document described how the pets were being disposed of by this facility. Unless it was "specially requested," and "paid to be cremated by their owners or by the veterinary clinic," these animals were rendered.

I checked back with Canadian veterinarians and found that not one of them was paying extra to have animals cremated. The standard fee (from $20 Canadian and more, depending on the size of the animal) was only for the disposal of the animal and this fee did not include cremation. Again, depending on the size of the animal, cremation could be an additional $20 Canadian and up. Private cremations, where the pet is cremated with no other animals, can cost $100 Canadian and more. Usually, a number of pets are cremated together and the ashes returned to the owners could be composed of not only their pet but other pets cremated at the same time. The only way you can be entirely sure that your pet is cremated is to be present at the cremation. Some companies will accommodate your request, others do not want owners present. If you are considering cremation, be sure to check all aspects of cremation prior to needing this service.

The document from the Canadian ministry noted that these animals were being shipped to a broker that was located about three hundred miles away. Again in 1992 I contacted the government investigator for the province of Ontario and asked what happened to the animals when they reached the broker. The investigator promptly replied, explaining that the broker's facility was just a stopping point for these animals. The broker's job is to find a renderer that pays the highest price. The investigator was kind enough to advise me what rendering plant the broker was selling to at that time. The plant was located in another province, Quebec.

In the 1990s, I was able to confirm that the path of the euthanized pet went from the veterinary clinic to the receiving plant, then to the broker, and finally, to the rendering plant where it was rendered and sold to feed mills and pet food companies.

Still not believing what I was hearing and reading, I contacted the Minister of Agriculture in Quebec where a number of the rendering plants are located. I asked that he confirm the truth of this practice. The Quebec minister wrote, "Dead animals are cooked together with viscera, bones and fats at 115° Celsius (C.) [230° Fahrenheit (F.)] for twenty minutes." Also, "The fur is not removed from dogs and cats."[8]

In later investigations in both the United States and Canada, I learned that the collars, tags, flea collars, and even the plastic bags in which the pets are wrapped, are not removed before they are shoved into the rendering vat. Deceased pets were and are being "recycled" into pet food unbeknownst to most pet owners.

In 1992, when I first notified veterinarians in Ontario as well as the general Canadian public via a live radio show explaining that euthanized pets were being sent to rendering facilities in Quebec, the public outcry was tremendous. Veterinarians immediately cancelled their contracts with the dead-stock removal company and the euthanized pets were sent to the local humane society, which operates a cremation facility.

Oops! Wrong Email Recipient

To give you an idea of how governments like to keep things under wraps, I'll share a frustrating yet funny incident. In June 2001, I wrote the Provincial Ministry of Agriculture to inquire if this particular dead-stock removal broker was still in operation. If so, was the broker still accepting euthanized dogs and cats and selling them to rendering plants in Quebec. Gerald Townsend, an employee with the ministry, passed my inquiry on to Tom Baker, DVM, who must have been with the ministry when I first began making inquiries about this particular broker in the mid-1990s.

Unknowingly, Dr. Baker mistakenly sent to me an email that was intended for Townsend. The email read: "Ms. Martin has a long history on this issue. She made staff life hell for several years. I recommend that we let her lie low and not respond further except in a very succinct manner."[9]

Dr. Baker mistakenly had hit the reply key and sent me the message. I then responded to Dr. Baker via email, informing him that he had sent the message to the wrong party! He did apologize, and did eventually forward the information I had requested. Yes, this particular gentleman is still the owner and was still operating as a broker. And no, the broker was no longer accepting euthanized dogs and cats for resale. Dr. Baker simply stated that pet food processors here in Ontario had a "long-term ban on cats and dogs as raw material."

Nine years after I found out that the euthanized animals from Ontario were being shipped to a rendering plant in Quebec, a reporter with Toronto's *Globe and Mail* confirmed this practice in a June 2001 article. Colin Freeze reported, "Quebec rendering giant Sanimal, Inc. recently told its suppliers, including shelters across the province that put down pets, that bowing to consumer sensibilities, it will no longer accept the carcasses of domestic pets."[10]

Philip Lee-Shanok, a reporter from the *Toronto Sun*, reported, "The protein meal is sold to various pet food manufacturers and other animal feed companies." When Lee-Shanok interviewed Mario Couture, Sanimal's head of procurement about euthanized pets rendered into pet food, he stated, "This food is healthy and good, but some people don't like to see meat meal that contains any pets."[11] (If you read the ingredient descriptions for pet food in Chapter One, it is doubtful that the food is healthy and good!)

Over the years I have learned that when one of these rendering operations ceases, another starts up and carries on. In June

2001, I again wrote to the Ministry of Agriculture in Quebec, advising the officials that I was aware that Sanimal, Inc. was no longer accepting companion animals for rendering. I asked, "Are you aware of any other rendering plants in Quebec that accept dogs and cats for rendering?" The reply I received from the office of the ministry was in French. The translation reads, "Here is the establishment that now accepts cats and dogs, Maple Leaf, Inc."[12] I have contacted this company a total of three times, the last time in late August 2002.

Once again I asked if it was Maple Leaf's policy to render companion animals. At the time of publication in Winter 2002, I still had not received a reply. The only information I could acquire on Maple Leaf, Inc. was from its Annual Information Form for 2001,which states the company owns six rendering plants in Canada and a pet food company, Shur-Gain, which is located in Quebec.

Testing for Cats and Dogs in Pet Food

Pet food companies deny that they use rendered animal companions, and clearly, some of them distance themselves from any connection to this practice. The official mouthpiece for the pet food industry in the United States, PFI, stands by its claim that the twenty-eight pet food companies it represents do not use by-products created from euthanized pets. However, despite PFI officials' claims, it is clear to me that pet food manufacturers do not conduct any tests to determine what are the sources of protein used in the meat meal they purchase. Until pet food manufacturers are willing to start testing the protein source, they will continue to be questioned by consumers—and certainly by me!

The FDA/CVM, as part of their study on sodium pentobarbital, which is discussed in Chapter Three, also stated that it "developed a test to detect dog and cat DNA in the protein of the dog food."[13] The FDA/CVM noted that all samples from its survey were examined for the remains derived from dogs and cats. The results showed a complete absence of material from euthanized dogs and cats.

On closer scrutiny, the FDA/CVM provides very little information in this report, including how the DNA testing was conducted. Under the U.S. Freedom of Information Act, I have requested all documentation related to these tests. Some of my unanswered questions include:

1) Can DNA survive the rendering process?

2) Can DNA survive the processing of the raw material, the "preconditioning state," where the raw material undergoes a steam process and extrusion (a kneading and cooking process)?

The FDA/CVM acknowledged my faxed request in March 2002. In June and again in August, I contacted the FDA/CVM with the Freedom of Information Act, and requested the status of my request. As of press time in Winter 2002, I still have not received a response.

I am suspicious of whether DNA testing *after* the rendering process can detect anything because of the destruction of DNA. Peter Faletra, PhD, explains how heat breaks the bonds between the two strands of DNA: "The cells of the organism are degraded by the heat, and that liberates enzymes, called DNAses that eat away the DNA. The cell destroys its own DNA when it is dying."[14]

Standard DNA identification depends on fresh blood samples or other non-degraded tissues. DNA cannot be attained when heat is involved. In DNA testing for cats and dogs in rendered and processed material there is neither fresh blood nor non-degraded tissues. Often, in rendering, the markers for the detection of the substance—in this case cat and dog—are eliminated during processing. Polymerase Chain Reaction (PCR) is a technique for the amplification of DNA; however, according to the FDA's report researchers did not use this method.

The fact that dogs and cats, or any other animals are difficult to detect in rendered material was confirmed in personal correspondence with Albert Harper, PhD, Director of the Henry C.

Lee Institute of Forensic Science. He wrote, "I think it would be very highly unlikely that identifiable DNA would survive the prolonged high temperatures associated with the manufacturing process of kibble. It is also highly unlikely that any species specific antigens would be present either. If the DNA testing you wrote about was conducted prior to heating the meats, then the testing would provide results."[15]

To find out more about DNA testing I went to some experts. No one seems sure of how the heat from rendering and processing affects DNA. Rainer Schubbert, DVM, from Medi Genomix in Germany noted, "In most products small amounts of DNA are still present, in some cases you need a lot of material to isolate enough DNA for analyses."[16] Dick Bowen from the Department of Biomedical Sciences, Colorado State University wrote, "Clearly, the heat used in rendering would destroy a lot of the DNA, but small pieces would probably survive, allowing detection (via PCR test)."[17]

A friend of mine, Gene Weddington, a retired chemist for a large rendering conglomerate in the United States, provided some insight into the rendering operation and the cooking system. "To understand this better simply think of it as a system where first in is first out with little blending taking place. If a plant received a large amount of companion animals during one day's operation it is possible that within the finished product there is a 'core' of almost pure rendered companion animals, this could possibly end up in a pet food account." He prefaced this by saying that he knew of no rendering plant in the United States that segregated companion animals from the rest of the material. [18]

THREE

Sodium Pentobarbital in Pet Food

Sodium pentobarbital is a barbiturate drug that veterinarians and animal shelters use to euthanize dogs and cats, but it can also be used on cattle and horses. Some of the brand names that include sodium pentobarbital are Sleepaway, Beuthanasia-D, Euthasol, Euthanasia-6, FP-3, Repose, and Fatal Plus.[1] Federal laws restrict the use of this drug and it can only be administered under the direction of a veterinarian.

In euthanasia, a veterinarian administers sodium pentobarbital intravenously, which causes a rapid death with minimal discomfort to the dying animal. Veterinarians consider this to be the most humane method for small animals.

As I discuss elsewhere, euthanized cats and dogs often end up in rendering vats along with other questionable material to make meat meal, and meat and bone meal. This can be problematic because sodium pentobarbital can withstand the heat from rendering. For years, some veterinarians and animal advocates have known about the potential danger of sodium pentobarbital residue in commercial pet food, yet the danger has not been alleviated. The "Report of the American Veterinary Medical Association (AVMA) Panel on Euthanasia," states, "In euthanasia of animals intended for human or animal food, chemical agents that result in tissue residue cannot be used."[2]

The AVMA report also states, "Carbon dioxide is the only chemical currently used in euthanasia of food animals that does not lead to tissue residues."[3] Sodium pentobarbital is listed by the AVMA as a noninhalant pharmaceutical chemical agent, which means it is a chemical agent that leaves a residue in the euthanized animal. Therefore, sodium pentobarbital would not be used to euthanize animals intended for food.

Research on Sodium Pentobarbital and Pet Food

Since first learning about the danger of sodium pentobarbital in pet food in 1995, I have searched many veterinary journals for more information. Basically, very little information or research is available on this topic. In 1995, three veterinarians from the University of Minnesota conducted an extensive study on the heat stability of sodium pentobarbital. The research concluded that sodium pentobarbital "survived rendering without undergoing degradation."[4] The study pointed to one case in which a dog exhibited pentobarbital toxicosis after eating the thoracic organs of a calf. Even after boiling the liver for twenty minutes, the levels of sodium pentobarbital had not decreased.

In addition, I have found nothing that determines what level of sodium pentobarbital can cause toxicity in a dog or cat. However, a 1998 report on feed safety from the United States Animal Health Association (USAHA), states, "Over the years, CVM has received sporadic reports of tolerance to pentobarbital in dogs. In 1996, the Center for Veterinary Medicine (CVM) developed and validated a method to detect pentobarbital in dry dog food and a preliminary survey of 10 samples found low levels in 2 samples. CVM had collected 75 representative dry dog food samples and were in the process of analyzing these for pentobarbital levels."[5]

I contacted a veterinarian with the FDA/CVM, Sharon Benz, eager to find out the results of these tests. Dr. Benz referred my inquiry to the Public Information Specialist, Linda Grassie. She advised me that the results of this study were to be posted on its website in the spring of 2000. For the next year I checked this site numerous times and contacted FDA/CVM several times, including the FDA Commissioner, Jane Henney, MD, and still nothing. Finally, Dr. Henney did write back, stating "The study is still ongoing and at this time we cannot estimate a completion date."[6]

Freedom of Information Act and the FDA

In May 2001, I filed a request under the Freedom of Information Act (FOIA) asking for the results of the first ten samples of the study, plus the subsequent seventy-five samples that were tested. In September 2001, I received a letter from Marilyn Broderick from the Office of Communication, Food and Drug Administration, Department of Health and Human Services as a result of my FOIA request. She provided information on the initial testing method used to determine the levels of sodium pentobarbital in dry dog food.

The letter stated, "The Center for Veterinary Medicine (CVM) began research in 1995 to develop a test method to detect pentobarbital residues in dog food. The procedure initially developed consisted of a qualitative analytical method."[7] This method was designed primarily to analyze pet food containing significant concentrations of "meat and bone meal" referred to as "MBM." (Note that meat and bone meal is composed of material from rendering plants.)

Broderick explained, "CVM developed this method [Gas Chromatography/Mass Spectrometry] on samples of pet food with label analysis percentages that fall within the following ranges: protein 17-32%; fat 6-20%; fiber 2-9%; moisture 10-30%. The pet foods tested during the method development study were A&P, Authority, Bil-Jac, Cycle, Deli-cat, Eukanuba, Hill's Science Diet, Iams, Ol'Roy and Purina."[8]

I asked in my FOIA request for the complete study that the FDA/CVM had undertaken on the dry commercial dog foods, which may have contained levels of sodium pentobarbital. Broderick's letter did not indicate which of the foods tested contained levels of this drug. In closing, Broderick wrote, "We request you wait until the evaluation process is complete, at which time we will send the full results to you. CVM expects that this will be ready by the end of January 2002."[9]

January 2002 came and went and nothing was posted. After more than two years of waiting, and contacting the FDA/CVM, it posted the results in March 2002.

Test Results from the FDA/CVM

During the 1990s, the FDA/CVM received reports from veterinarians complaining that when they used sodium pentobarbital as an anesthetizing agent for dogs, the drug seemed to be losing its effectiveness. Based on these reports, CVM officials decided to investigate a plausible theory that the dogs were exposed to pentobarbital through dog food, and that this exposure was making the dogs less responsive to pentobarbital when it was used as a drug. The researchers surmised that sodium pentobarbital was finding its way into commercial pet foods through animals who had been euthanized with this drug and rendered for use as a "meat meal" in pet food.

In conjunction with this study, the FDA/CVM wanted to determine if pet foods contained rendered remains of dogs and cats.[10] Basically, this was a two-part study. In 1998 and again in 2000 scientists from the FDA/CVM purchased dry dog foods from retail outlets near its facilities in Laurel, Maryland.

Only dog foods with certain animal-derived ingredients were sampled. This included products containing meal and bone meal (MBM), animal digest (AD), animal fat (AF), and beef and bone meal (BBM)—all of which would be derived from euthanized animals. The report indicates that the products listed near the top of the ingredients on the labels, would be more likely to contain sodium pentobarbital than those ingredients listed near the bottom.

According to the FDA/CVM, "In survey #1 two different lots for the same formulation were sampled in 37 cases, making up 74 samples. The different lots gave the same results in only 31 of 37 cases."[11] The reason for the variation was because the composition of the raw material may vary, even if the formulations do not. Researchers analyzed the samples to determine if sodium pentobarbital was present.

In the first survey conducted in 1998, researchers found the presence of sodium pentobarbital in the foods listed below although the levels of this drug were unknown.

1. Super G—Chunk Style
2. Pet Essentials—Chunk Style
3. America's Choice—Krunchy Kibble
4. Weis Value—Crunchy Dog Food
5. Weis Value—Gravy Style Dog Food
6. Weis Value—High Protein Dog Food
7. Ol' Roy—Meaty Chunks and Gravy
8. Ken-L Ration—Gravy Train Beef, Liver and Bacon Flavor
9. Ken-L Ration—Gravy Train
10. Heinz—Kibbles 'n Bits Jerky
11. Weis Value—Kibbles Variety Mix
12. Kibble Select—Premium Dog Food
13. Nutro—Premium
14. Ol' Roy—Krunchy Bites & Bones
15. Ol' Roy—Premium Formula with Chicken Protein and Rice
16. Ol' Roy—High Performance with Chicken Protein and Rice
17. Trailblazer—Chunk Premium Quality
18. Trailblazer—Bite Size Ration
19. Dad's—Bite Size Meal
20. Weis Value—Chunky and Moist
21. Weis Value—Puppy Food
22. Super G—Chunk Style
23. Richfood—Chunk Style
24. Richfood—Gravy Style Dog Food
25. Heinz—Kibbles 'n Bits Puppy
26. Champ Chunx—Bite Size Dog Food
27. Heinz—Kibbles 'n Bits Lean
28. ProPlan—Beef and Rice Adult
29. ProPlan—Beef and Rice Puppy
30. Reward—Dinner Rounds Dog Food

In the FDA/CVM survey #2 conducted in December 2000, researchers analyzed only one lot of each formulation. In this second survey, other samples were analyzed to measure how much pentobarbital might be present.

Survey #2 did show the levels of sodium pentobarbital in parts per billion (ppb). Parts per billion are considered to be minute amounts of any substance which, through testing methods, can be found in solids and liquids.

1. Old Roy—Puppy Formula, beef flavor, 10.0 ppb.
2. Old Roy—Puppy Formula, chicken and rice, 32.0 ppb.
3. Richfood—High Protein Dog Meal, 3.9 ppb.
4. Weis—Total High Energy Chicken and Rice, 15.0 ppb.
5. Old Roy—Lean Formula, 3.9 ppb.
6. Super G—Gravy Style Dog Food, 4.5 ppb.
7. Super G—Chunk Style Dog Food, 16.4 ppb.
8. Heinz—Kibbles 'n Bits Beefy Bits, 25.1 ppb.
9. Dad's—Bite Size Meal Chicken and Rice, 8.4 ppb.
10. Pet Gold—Master Diet Puppy Formulation, 11.6 ppb.

The FDA/CVM noted that although some pet food formulations did test positive for sodium pentobarbital levels, they might be free of this drug now. Every lot of rendered material is composed of various animal tissues. Therefore, if the animals rendered today are cattle who have died in the field or roadkill, there would be no levels of sodium pentobarbital detected. If the rendered material was composed of dogs, cats, cattle, and horses euthanized with sodium pentobarbital, this would be detected in the food.

Also, the FDA has no way to know whether pet food brands that were not sampled had pentobarbital residue. The FDA/CVM admitted in the report that ingredient sources vary geographically. "Feed manufacturers have regional ingredient suppliers and manufacturing facilities. Samples available in a specific geographical region may not reflect the nation as a whole. Ingredient sources for pet foods vary based on such considerations as availability and cost."[12]

I was amazed to learn that with the extent and the length of this undertaking that samples were not obtained from various regions in the United States to provide a better perspective of which foods did contain sodium pentobarbital. Many of the foods tested are from samples of private label or generic foods. I am sure many consumers, myself included, would rather see more testing done on foods produced by the large multinational pet food companies, rather than the smaller, regional outfits.

In the same study the FDA/CVM undertook DNA testing on the same dry commercial dog foods to see if any contained the remains of euthanized dogs and cats. The results of these tests are discussed in Chapter Two.

Another Test Determines Risk of Sodium Pentobarbital

The FDA/CVM undertook an assessment of the risk dogs might face if ingesting sodium pentobarbital in pet food. The report did not divulge how many dogs were used in the study or how the drug was administered. This is information I hope to acquire if the FDA/CVM supplies me with the complete report, which I have requested under FOIA.

The report simply states that the dogs were each given either 50, 150, or 500 mg, of pentobarbital for eight weeks. The results were compared with control animals who were not given sodium pentobarbital. Several significant pentobarbital associated effects were identified in this study:

- Dogs who received 150 and 500 mg. pentobarbital once daily for eight weeks had statistically higher liver weights (relative to their bodyweights) than the animals in the control groups. Increased liver weights are associated with the increased production by the liver of cytochrome P450 enzymes;

- An analysis showed that the activity of at least three liver enzymes was statistically greater than that of the controls at doses of approximately 200 mg. pentobarbital per day or greater.[13]

Increased liver enzymes can indicate a serious problem. The liver performs many functions—detoxifying poisons and drugs, digestion and formation of proteins, fats and sugars, manufacturing bile, and assisting in blood clotting, to name a few. The prime symptom that indicates liver disease is jaundice, which presents as yellowing of the skin, mucous membranes, and whites of the eyes. Other symptoms may include lack of appetite, weight loss, depression, vomiting, diarrhea, increased thirst, urination, and an enlarged abdomen. The only way to ascertain if liver disease is involved is to have a complete workup on your pet that includes a liver function test.

The researchers found no statistical difference in relative liver weight or liver enzyme activity between the group receiving 50 mg. pentobarbital per day or none at all in the control group. The researchers also assumed that most dogs would be exposed to no more than four mg./kg. body weight per day, based on the highest level of sodium pentobarbital found in the survey of dog foods.

Study Conclusion

The conclusion of the study is that it is unlikely that a dog consuming dry dog food would experience any adverse effects from the low levels found in these foods, and that these levels are "probably safe." (Keep in mind that our pets eat these foods on a daily basis for many years. This study lasted eight weeks.)

Animal Ark, a no-kill shelter in Minnesota, posed some important questions after FDA/CVM published the results of this test. "The FDA test did not check for possible interactions with other drugs," noted Animal Ark. "They did not test for possible interactions with other common chemicals found in pet foods. The FDA measured a single liver enzyme. They then sought to find the minimal daily dose that did not elevate this enzyme. While it may be true (no one knows) that this enzyme is a good indicator of the overall effect this drug has on the body, it certainly is not the only potential indicator. Clearly other effects could be occurring that would not be measured by this one enzyme."[14]

The FDA acknowledges that had these levels of drugs been found in human food, an instant recall would have been mandated and production of the food stopped.

Does the FDA Allow Sodium Pentobarbital in Pet Food?

The FDA's study confirmed that sodium pentobarbital is finding its way into pet foods from rendered euthanized animals. At the same time, the U.S. Code of Federal Regulations, titled "FDA Approved Animal Drug Products," clearly states, "Do not use in animals intended for food."

It was my assumption that this regulation applies to food for humans and animals. To clarify this point I contacted various government agencies. Stephen Sundlof, DVM, Director of the FDA's Center for Veterinary Medicine, referred me to Linda Grassie, FDA's Public Information Specialist. (In the past, Grassie and I had communicated on several other issues.) Grassie clarified that when sodium pentobarbital was approved in 1980 it was approved for euthanasia in dogs. Therefore, the FDA believes that at the time of approval the phrase, "Do not use in animals intended for food," applied to non-human food use of these animals since dogs were not considered food animals."[15]

Grassie also explained that the Animal Medicinal Drug Use Clarification Act (AMDUCA) has allowed extra label use (meaning it can be used on other animals) of products provided they do not result in a tissue residue. Extra label use is also allowed if there is a sufficient withdrawal time prior to slaughter to ensure that a harmful tissue residue does not exist in edible product. Grassie also noted, "A euthanasia solution such as pentobarbital obviously cannot have a withdrawal time and its mechanism of action results in a tissue residue so it could not be used to euthanize animals intended for human or animal food."[16]

What I have concluded is that the FDA/CVM under its regulations does not allow animals injected with sodium pentobarbital to be used in pet food product. At the same time, the FDA also confirmed after the testing conducted by the FDA/CVM that sodium pentobarbital indeed is in the thirty pet foods they tested. Therefore, in many cases commercial pet food companies are not following FDA regulations, the FDA knows this, yet, the FDA has not taken any action to stop this practice.

Sodium Pentobarbital and Large Animals

The FDA stated that the sodium pentobarbital it found in the dry commercial foods tested came from large animals, cattle, and horses. In order to find out if this was a drug of choice for euthanasia of large animals, I contacted four veterinarians who oversee departments of agriculture. I asked them if they euthanize large animals with sodium pentobarbital, and if so, are the animals processed for human or animal food?

Wayne E. Cunningham, DVM, SM, a Colorado State Veterinarian, replied, "Any animal euthanized with pentobarbital is not allowed into human or the pet food chain."[17] Leroy Coffman, the state veterinarian for Florida was in agreement with Dr. Cunningham: "FDA regulation prohibits the use of any animal euthanized with sodium pentobarbital from being used in the human or animal food chain."[18] Wayne Flory, DVM, from Texas A&M University responded that sodium pentobarbital may be used to euthanize some cattle and horses, however, he noted, "These animals are restricted from being rendered and used as a source of protein for cat and dog food."[19]

In Canada, Helene Chagon, DVM, with the Canadian Government, Veterinary Products, responded to my query stating, "Several products containing sodium pentobarbital have been approved for use in Canada as euthanasia agents for small and large animals, including cattle and horses. However, euthanized animals should not be used in animal feeds."[20]

It is clear by the response from these veterinarians that animals euthanized with drugs containing sodium pentobarbital should not be used for human or animal consumption.

The Dangers of Sodium Pentobarbital and Wild Life

Farm animals who are euthanized with sodium pentobarbital must be carefully disposed of because other animals may be at risk. Lori Miser, DVM, from the Illinois Department of Agriculture, wrote, "Bald and golden eagles as well as dogs, cats, and a wide variety of zoo animals have died after consuming animal parts from animals euthanized with common euthanasia solutions-secondary sodium pentobarbital toxicosis."[21]

In "Euthanasia of Horses," an information sheet published by the California Department of Food and Agriculture, Animal Health and Food, it is very clear that proper disposal of a euthanized carcass is imperative. It warns: "After barbiturate overdoses, the carcass of the horse will be unfit for human or animal consumption.... Keep in mind that house pets and wildlife that ingest portions of the barbiturate-injected carcass can be poisoned."[22]

Perhaps the most compelling information on the dangers of sodium pentobarbital comes from the National Euthanasia Registry, a continuing education program of the Raptor Education Foundation. This is a nonprofit organization in Colorado devoted to the education of veterinarians about the dangers involved in large animal euthanasia. Raptors include eagles, hawks, falcons, owls, kites, osprey, and harriers. Many of these birds have been poisoned after eating animals euthanized with sodium pentobarbital. This can happen because ranchers have not buried cattle immediately after death or have buried them in shallow graves. The birds can also be poisoned when shelters dump euthanized dogs and cats in landfill sites and the birds feed on these carcasses. Sodium pentobarbital remains potent in a carcass long after the animal dies.

A January 2002 publication by the American Veterinary Medical Association describes some of the deaths of wildlife related to sodium pentobarbital. "In British Columbia, 26 bald eagles became ill, five fatally, after eating one euthanized cow."[23] A Colorado case in 1999, involved five golden eagles and two bald eagles who died after ingesting the carcasses of two mules euthanized with sodium pentobarbital. Although accidental, the veterinarian and rancher involved in the these cases were ordered to pay $10,000 for involuntarily killing the seven birds. "These broad-winged fliers are protected under the Migratory Bird Treaty Act, Eagle Protection Act, and Endangered Species Act," writes Kate O'Rourke from the AVMA. "Maximal fines for killing a bald eagle or another bird protected by the EPA or ESA can run as high as $100,000 for an individual and $200,000 for an organization."[24]

Raptors are not the only wildlife suffering secondary sodium pentobarbital toxicosis. The National Euthanasia Registry cites a case reported by Terry Grosz, a retired U.S. Fish and Wildlife Service agent. His report states, "A hungry mother grizzly coming out of her den, with two cubs to feed, smelled a decaying carcass and dug down through ten feet of earth to get at the meat. She and her cubs died."[25]

Who is to blame for the deaths of these and other animals who have ingested carcasses euthanized with sodium pentobarbital? The veterinarian who administers these drugs? The ranch or veterinary clinic that does not bury or dispose of the carcasses in the proper manner? Or the pharmaceutical companies that do not have proper warnings on their products?

Ft. Dodge Animal Health is the manufacturer of the euthanasia agent Sleepaway, which was the drug that killed the seven eagles. When the National Euthanisia Registry asked Ft. Dodge Animal Health who should carry the burden of responsibility, the manufacturer officially responded: "It was simply not our responsibility, besides there really wasn't any profit in the drug anyway."[26]

Although these drugs containing sodium pentobarbital provide a humane means of killing an animal, something must be done to prevent sodium pentobarbital from killing other animals who might ingest carcasses.

Long-Term Effects

We don't know the long-term effects of sodium pentobarbital ingested in small amounts over many years. If indeed, as the FDA confirmed in its study, sodium pentobarbital exists in small quantities in most of the pet foods it tested, and animal companions eat these foods regularly—what might be the adverse effects over years of exposure?

It seems the only way we can prevent this drug from being passed on to other animals, via rendering or improper burial, is to have all animals who are euthanized with any drugs containing sodium pentobarbital to be cremated or incinerated. And in the case of large animals euthanized with sodium pentobarbital, there must be immediate removal of the body before other animals feed off of the carcasses. Ultimately, I believe the FDA must enforce its regulations regarding sodium pentobarbital.

– *Four* –

Pet Food Regulations

For many years I assumed commercial pet food, and the many ingredients that went into it, were closely regulated by a government body, most likely the Department of Agriculture. Once I began asking questions, I soon learned a very different reality. I was amazed to find out that although on the surface it sounds like this is a well-regulated industry, looks can be deceiving.

Over the years, I have spoken to many pet owners about the dangers of commercial pet foods. In the beginning, every single pet owner was positive that the government closely regulates the industry. One pet-supply owner became incensed when I told him that this was an unregulated industry. He was convinced that a government agency inspected every piece of meat and grain put into pet food. There was a time when I believed that too.

Since I am Canadian, I first approached our Provincial Ministry of Agriculture in 1991 about pet food regulation in Canada. I learned that the "Labeling Act," only states that the pet food label must contain the name and address of the company, the weight of the product, and if it is made for a dog or cat. No other Canadian regulations exist. That was, and continues to be, the extent of government regulation of pet foods in Canada as of 2002.

Since the vast majority of pet food sold in Canada is imported from the United States, I then turned to the United States to find out about regulations and what government agencies are involved. At first, I assumed that the U.S. Department of Agriculture, Animal and Plant Health Inspection Services (USDA/APHIS) is involved. I found out that this agency only administers the Animal Welfare Act that deals with minimum standards of humane care and treatment of animals sold into the pet trade, transported commercially, exhibited to the public, and used in research. This agency does not have any input into ingredients or regulations as they pertain to commercial pet food.

Next, I contacted the U. S. Department of Agriculture, Food Safety and Inspection Service (USDA/FSIS) to see if this agency was involved with regulations of the pet food industry. I learned that its responsibility relates to meat for human consumption only. Its mandate is to insure that meat and poultry are safe, wholesome, and accurately labeled.

Eventually, I learned that there are basically three organizations that oversee the pet foods sold in the United States: The Food and Drug Administration, Center for Veterinary Medicine (FDA/CVM); Association of American Feed Control Officials (AAFCO); and Pet Food Institute (PFI).

USDA oversees pet food sold outside of the country. However, the so-called regulations of the pet food industry in the United States are complex and convoluted. For example, animal feed, which includes livestock and pet food, falls under the jurisdiction of the FDA/CVM; however, AAFCO sets the guidelines for the labeling of pet food. In the end, it is up to each state to choose whether or not it will even adopt these guidelines. All of these guidelines are ultimately voluntary.

The FDA/CVM and Pet Food Regulation

What entity in the government bureaucracy actually oversees and regulates pet food production in the United States? Basically, it is the Food and Drug Administration, Center for Veterinary Medicine (FDA/CVM) based in Washington, D.C. FDA regulations apply to food, drugs, medical devices, cosmetics, vaccines, blood products, and radiation-emitting products (cell phones, lasers, microwaves)—all products related to human use.

The Center for Veterinary Medicine (CVM), a division of the FDA, deals with animals. The regulations, as they apply to dogs and cats, primarily regulate the manufacture and distribution of food additives and drugs for pets. The CVM has no input as to the sources of protein, carbohydrates, or fats used in pet foods. It also oversees labeling and health claims made about a pet food.

If your dog or cat becomes ill after eating a pet food manufactured in the United States, can you go to the FDA/CVM and request that this government agency investigate? Unless you can provide scientific data that indicates the source of the problem, the answer is no. FDA/CVM requires chemical analysis of the food, veterinary reports, any blood work, urinalysis, or any other medical tests done on your pet, which can be very costly for a consumer. Then, and only then, will the FDA investigate.

The role of the FDA/CVM in overseeing the safety and nutritional value of pet food is stated simply and directly in its "Information for Consumers" bulletin. The FDA/CVM states that under the Federal Food, Drug, and Cosmetic Act, "the Center for Veterinary Medicine is responsible for the regulation of animal drugs, medicated feeds, food additives, and feed ingredients, including pet foods." The bulletin goes on to state that "the Act does require that pet foods, like human foods, be pure and wholesome, contain no harmful or deleterious substances, and be truthfully labeled."[1]

Given this clear mission stated by the FDA/CVM in its consumer bulletin that goes out to thousands of individuals, I wondered exactly how this was accomplished. Did the FDA/CVM actually test commercial pet foods to ascertain if they are indeed pure and wholesome and contain no harmful ingredients? Are there inspectors, appointed by the FDA/CVM, physically present in commercial pet food plants to inspect the composition of the ingredients used?

I posed these questions to the CVM. Once again I heard from Linda Grassie, spokesperson for CVM. She had forwarded my questions to the CVM's Division of Animal Feeds for reply. "Due to their large volume of work, they answer requests from the public in the order they are received," Grassie explained in her written correspondence. "I understand that this may take some time, quite possibly 90 days."[2] Well, in the past twelve years of asking for information from various government agencies in the United States and in Canada, I have grown accustomed to waiting. In some cases it has taken more than two years. (See the sodium pentobarbital controversy discussed in Chapter Three.) As of November 2002, I have never received a reply to my original question: Does the FDA/CVM test commercial pet foods to ascertain if they are indeed pure and wholesome and contain no harmful ingredients?

The main focus of the FDA/CVM revolves around verifying health claims made by pet food companies rather than investigating consumer complaints about pet food. The FDA/CVM oversees health claims made by pet food companies placed on their labels to attract consumers to their particular product. Pet food companies are not supposed to make claims that their particular pet food is for the prevention or treatment of a disease. For example, in 1990 some pet food manufacturers advertised that their cat food might prevent Feline Urological Syndrome (FUS). This is a drug claim that the FDA/CVM challenged as false. The pet food manufacturers were given ample time to remove bags of pet food with this false claim and change labels, deleting the claim. When some manufacturers did not comply, the FDA and state officials seized hundreds of tons of cat food. One company, whose products were seized, assured the FDA that the product would no longer be labeled for the prevention of FUS and sold in the United States. However, this does not mean that the pet food company cannot continue to sell their product with the false claim in other countries without regulations—Canada, for one.

AAFCO and Pet Food Regulations

The FDA works in partnership with the Association of American Feed Control Officials (AAFCO) and a representative from the FDA/CVM serves on the Board of Directors of AAFCO. However, AAFCO is not a government agency but an organization. AAFCO's literature states that it is an organization "in which officials of state, provincial, dominion and federal agencies, engage in the regulation of production, analysis, labeling, distribution and sale of animal feeds and livestock remedies, may exchange ideas and share experience for mutual benefit and development of uniformity."[3]

It is also interesting to note that although the literature from AAFCO states that this organization is composed of employees of state, federal, and provincial agencies, its membership directory includes representation from a number of pet food companies. Members include Heinz Pet Foods, Bil Jac Pet Foods, Nutramax, Purina, the Iams Company, Nutro, Kal Kan Foods, and American Nutrition Inc., a company that makes a number of no-name or store-brand pet foods. The roster also includes members from the rendering industry and the Pet Food Institute (PFI).

AAFCO and Feed Analysis

One of AAFCO's undertakings is a sample feed program for feed analysis. This is conducted primarily on livestock feed but may include pet food. What does this analytical testing entail? According to the Department of Agriculture, State of Colorado, their testing includes "Protein, fat, fiber, moisture, ash, calcium, phosphorus and salt, which are compared monthly."[4]

If the label states 22 percent protein, 8 percent fat, 2.5 percent fiber, then it must contain those levels. The sources of these proteins, fats, and fiber do not matter. The pet food could contain road kill, zoo animals, or slaughterhouse waste as sources of protein. Fats can be obtained from restaurant fryers or the rendering process, and fiber could include peanut hulls or beet pulp (the residue of the sugar beet harvest). Someone once wrote cynically that these levels of protein, fats, and fiber can be achieved by combining old shoe leather, crankshaft oil, and sawdust. Because of financial restraints, most states only test livestock feed. Only eight states out of the fifty that I contacted actually test pet food.

AAFCO and Feeding Trials

Another aspect of pet food that AAFCO oversees is the feeding trials. A typical feeding trial uses eight dogs over one year of age. All the dogs must be of normal weight and health. Prior to the start of the trial all dogs must pass a physical examination. Their general health, body, and coat are evaluated. At the end of the trial four blood values are measured and recorded. They include hemoglobin, packed cell volume, serum alkaline phosphates, and serum albumin.

For six months the dogs are only fed the food being tested. In order for the dogs to finish the test, they must not lose more than 15 percent of their body weight. In addition, in order for the test to be valid, according to AAFCO standards, six of the eight dogs starting the feeding trial must finish the test and the dogs cannot lose more than 15 percent of their starting body weight. That is the complete criteria for AAFCO feeding trials. (Some pet food companies also conduct their own research or have an independent company test their foods. Such testing is discussed later in this chapter.)

In my opinion, AAFCO's feeding trials are inadequate and limited in scope, oversimplifying the acceptable test results and limiting the feeding trials to only eight dogs. In addition, the feeding trials only last a matter of months and give no indication of how these foods might affect animal companions who eat commercial foods for years.

The Pet Food Institute

The Pet Food Institute (PFI) is the official mouthpiece for pet food manufacturers in the United States and Canada. In order to belong to PFI, you must be a commercial pet food manufacturer. According to PFI's literature it is "the [pet food] industry's public and media relations resource, representative before the U.S. Congress and state and federal agencies, organizer of seminars and educational programs, sponsor and clearing-house for research, and liaison with other private organizations."

Over the years I have communicated with the executive director of PFI, Duane Ekedahl, and the Vice President of Technical and Regulatory Affairs, Nancy Cook. There is one question I have posed to them on numerous occasions, and Ekedahl and Cook have never answered it: "Do any of the pet food companies actually test the raw material to see if it contains rendered companion animals?"

I keep asking this question because PFI emphatically denies that any of its members use rendered companion animals in their products. According to a letter I received from Cook, "Please be advised that members of the Pet Food Institute, which represents 95% of the pet food produced in the United States, have taken steps to assure that no such ingredients are used in their products."[5] However, despite this reassurance, PFI has never outlined what steps have been taken by the pet food companies to assure pet owners that companion animals are not in commercial pet foods.

In January 2002, once again I wrote and asked Ekedahl and Cook to advise what testing the pet food industry actually conducts on its raw material. As of my publication deadline in November 2002, I have not received a reply.

In its information sheets PFI assures consumers that the United States Department of Agriculture (USDA) is involved at the federal level. "Pet food is regulated by the Food and Drug Administration (FDA), the states through their feed laws and the Association of American Feed Control Officials (AAFCO), and the U.S. Department of Agriculture (USDA)."[6]

Wanting to be reassured of the USDA's involvement, I contacted the USDA and inquired what role this government department played in the regulation of commercial pet foods. Denise Spencer, DVM, replied: "The USDA does not regulate pet food manufactured in the U.S., the FDA has this regulatory authority."[7] Dr. Spencer did note that pet foods are generally the same for domestic and foreign markets (same food, different packaging) and that her department, National Center for Import and Export, was only involved in inspecting pet food for export. The level of inspection was limited to checking that the product is free of certain diseases. There are different regulations for different countries regarding pet food ingredients.

Pet Food Regulations in Canada

The Canadian Veterinary Medical Association (CVMA) is a voluntary organization that certifies the pet foods produced in Canada. Most of these foods are brands found in the supermarket. The federal government is only responsible for the labeling of pet foods. The product must contain the name and address of the company, weight of the product, and if it is made for a dog or cat—nothing more.

Pet foods imported into Canada must be free of bovine spongiform encephalopathy (BSE), as well as free of foot and mouth disease. Porcine origin foods (pigs and swine) must be free of foot and mouth disease, swine vesicular disease, (a viral disease affecting pigs), African swine fever, and classical swine fever (hog cholera). If the pet food contains poultry products, the product must be free of Velogenic Newcastle disease, (characterized by lesions in the brain or gastrointestinal tract with mortality rates as high as 90 percent in susceptible chickens), and pathogenic influenza (fowl plague).

Foods that are considered to be safe "low-risk" foods, include, "Cooked, canned, commercially prepared pet food containing animal by-products (bone meal, meat meal, blood meal, rendered animal fats, glue stock, meat, inedible meat)."[8] For pet chews and treats shipped from the United States to Canada, the only requirement that the Canadian Food Inspection Agency requires, is "proof of origin [country of origin]."

Pet Food Regulations for Export to Europe

Most of the large U.S. pet food companies that have an overseas market also have their own facilities in that country and that is where the food is made. The regulations for pet food exported to Europe are far more stringent than those of other countries. High-risk materials that are considered unsafe for use in pet foods shipped to Europe include:

(a) All bovine animals, pigs, goats, sheep, solipeds, poultry and all other animals kept for agricultural production, which have died on the farm but were not slaughtered for human consumption, including stillborn and unborn animals;

(b) dead animals not referred to in point (a) but which are designated by the competent authority of the Member State;

(c) animals which are killed in the context of disease control measures either on the farm or in any other place designated by the competent authority;

(d) animal waste including blood originating from animals which show, during the veterinary inspection carried out at the time of slaughtering, clinical signs of disease communicable to man or other animals;

(e) all those parts of an animal slaughtered in the normal way which are not presented for post-mortem inspection, with the exception of hides, skin, hooves, feathers, wool, horns, blood and similar products;

(f) all meat, poultry meat, fish, game and foodstuffs or animal origin which are spoiled and thus present a risk to human and animal health;

(g) animals, fresh meat, poultry meat, fish, game and meat and milk products, imported for third countries, which in the course of the inspection provided for in community legislation fail to comply with the veterinary requirements for their importation into the Community, unless they are re-exported or their import is accepted under restrictions laid down in Community provisions;

(h) without prejudice to instances of emergency slaughtering for reasons of welfare, farm animals which have died in transit;

(i) animal waste containing residues of substances which may pose a danger to human or animal health; milk, meat or products of animal origin rendered unfit for human consumption by the presence of such residues;

(j) fish which show clinical signs of diseases communicable to man or fish.[9]

Pet Food Regulations in the United Kingdom

In the United Kingdom the organization that oversees the pet food industry is much like the Pet Food Institute in the United States. The Pet Food Manufacturers' Association (PFMA) represents approximately 95 percent of the U.K. pet food manufacturing industry and is comprised of fifty-six member companies. Its role is to promote pet food products, responsible pet ownership, represent its members' views to United Kingdom and European Union government departments, and raise standards in the pet food industry.

If you believe PFMA's literature, than the policies in the United Kingdom are much stricter than that of other countries. "Member companies only use materials from animal species which are generally accepted in the human food chain," states Alison Walker, spokesperson for PFMA. "This rules out the use of any materials from horses, ponies, whales and other sea mammals, kangaroos and many other species. The pet food industry only uses materials of beef, lamb, poultry and pork origin, fish, shellfish, rabbit and game."[10]

The literature further states that PFMA members use only materials derived from animals who have been inspected and passed as fit for human consumption. Most of the material derived from these animals would be listed on the labels as meat by-products. I questioned PFMA about the pet foods that are imported to the United Kingdom because of the dubious ingredients used in some of these products. Walker replied to my inquiry stating, "The import certification relates to materials specifically allowed in pet food—e.g., low risk materials or in other words that which is fit for, but not intended for, human consumption."[11] Walker also advised me that it is illegal to use dead companion animals in the manufacter of pet food in the United Kingdom and the rest of Europe. Although this may be true, still, in the United States and Canada there are no regulations that prohibit this material from being used in commercial pet food.

PFMA leaves it to the member companies to operate their own in-house quality assurance programs and feeding trials. Pet food manufacturers are also in charge of testing the incoming raw materials used in their products. Because of the number of cases of Bovine Spongiform Encaphalopathy (BSE) in the United Kingdom, and the nearly ninety cats who have died from the feline form of this disease as of March 2002, certain materials derived from beef have been banned for use in pet food. This includes the head, spleen, thymus, tonsils, brain, and spinal cord, and the large and small intestines of cows as well as sheep or goats. It is still legal to use pigs in pet foods because there have been no known cases of spongiform encephalopathy in these animals.

Pet Food Regulations in Japan

Like most countries the pet food industry in Japan is self-regulated. These self-regulations apply primarily to the labeling of the foods. The label must state if it is made for a dog or cat, the country of origin, the manufacturer, the distributor or importer, and a list of ingredients.

In Japan, fish meal is the only item mentioned in its regulations for pet food. It simply states that the processing plants for fish meal can only process this commodity. No other animals, including cattle, pigs, sheep, etc., can be processed at these plants.

The commercial pet food market in Japan has grown enormously in the last fifteen to twenty years. According to *The Japanese Market News,* a publication that provides statistics on various industries in Japan, the Japanese have an estimated ten million dogs and seven million cats as house pets. Japan imports most of its pet food. "Over 90 percent of imports have traditionally come from three countries: the United States, Australia, and Thailand, all three of which have abundant supplies of livestock and seafood [which compose the raw materials for pet food]," reports *The Japanese Market News.* [12]

An interesting aside, tastes in pet food appear to mirror a particular culture's eating habits. For example, fish-flavored cat food is preferred in Japan, while chicken-flavored cat food is more popular in Europe and North America. Japanese cats are traditionally fed leftovers such as fish heads and mashed fish plus leftover rice; therefore the Japanese assume that fish is a natural diet for felines.

Limited Regulations Internationally

It is clear that there are no government agencies in the United States, Canada, the United Kingdom, or Japan that actually regulate the raw ingredients used in commercial pet foods. The voluntary organizations, AAFCO, and CVMA that set standards for the industry, have no hard and fast enforcement standards. The logos of these organizations, which are displayed on pet food labels, simply mean that the products meet the minimum standard for nutrition, nothing more.

– *FIVE* –

Pet Food Manufacturers

The inspiration for pet food is attributed to an Ohio electrician, James Spratt, around 1860. Spratt traveled to England and while there noticed how pet owners fed their dogs leftover biscuits. This piqued his interest. Spratt decided that he could concoct a better biscuit for dogs from wheat, vegetables, beet root, and meat. Spratt ended up becoming a long-term resident of England, and sold his Dog Cakes in the United Kingdom until 1890 when a public company bought his formula and began operations in the United States. Spratt continued producing the Dog Cakes in the United Kingdom and his London factory was one of the largest dog food production operations in the world.

Other U.S. firms entered the pet food market in the 1920s using various formulas for dry biscuits and kibble. After World War I, pet food manufacturers introduced canned horsemeat for dog food. By 1930 pet food companies introduced canned food and dry meat-meal dog foods, but for the most part people still fed their pets leftovers from the dinner table. In subsequent years as farm machinery replaced teams of horses, horsemeat products became less plentiful, and meat and cereal by-products replaced horsemeat as the primary ingredients in pet food.

By the 1960s a great diversification in the types of pet food flourished. Manufacturers produced dry cat food, many more canned products, and soft-moist products. Various diets, including puppy formulas, "lite" foods, and life-stage diets filled the grocery store shelves, surpassing even cereal products for humans. Slaughterhouses, rendering plants, and cereal producers saw pet foods as the ideal product for their industries' by-products unfit for human consumption.

Today, pet food is a multi-billion dollar industry, and still growing. According to *Euromonitor*, a major market profiler, "Combined U.S. sales of dog and cat food reached a size of $11.6 billion in 2000."[1] Aside from the question of whether most commercial pet foods are healthy for cats and dogs, the industry itself continues to thrive and grow.

Multinational Pet Food Companies

Many of the small pet food companies were swallowed up by the large multinationals beginning in the 1950s and 1960s. For many years Mars, the maker of candy bars, has been one of the largest pet food companies in the world. Mars produces Pedigree dog food, Sheba and Whiskas cat food, and Waltham, which produces prescription diets that are sold primarily in veterinary clinics.

In 1968 Mars acquired Kal Kan, a company that dates back to 1936 when Clement L. Hirsch founded what was then Dog Town Packing Company.[2] Kal Kan continues to be at the same location in Vernon, California since the acquisition. Prior to that, Kal Kan had established an international presence with the Waltham Center for Pet Nutrition in England in 1965. In 2001 Mars purchased Royal Canin in France, further expanding its international reach and consolidating its lead in the European pet food market. Royal Canin produces a line of dry cat and dog foods, Natural Blend, Sensible Choice, Excel, and Kasco.[3]

Heinz, the ketchup maker, is also well known within the pet food industry. It produces Gravy Train, 9 Lives, Cycle, Kibbles 'n Bits, Reward, and Skippy. In 1996 Heinz acquired two pet food companies, one in Canada and the other in the United States. The Canadian Company, Martin Feed Mill Limited, had operated out of a small town in Ontario for many years producing dog, cat, and livestock feed. Martin's produced Techni-Cal and Medi-Cal, and the latter sold through veterinary clinics. Also in 1996,

Heinz acquired Nature's Recipe, a California-based company that produces specialty foods for dogs and cats. Nature's specialties include a hair ball formula, a urinary-health diet for cats, and an allergy diet for dogs.

In 1999, one of the largest and most unlikely mergers on record took place when Proctor and Gamble, makers of consumer products such as Tide, Bold, Vicks, and Puffs, purchased Iams for $2.3 billion. A self-educated animal nutritionist, Paul Iams, had founded his company in 1946, and produced Eukanuba, and Iams dry and canned dog and cat food.

The new owners, Procter and Gamble, announced that Iams—once sold in specialty stores and veterinary clinics—has a new goal: "Iams is sending its sales reps on a mission to make Iams available everywhere P&G's are sold. That is likely to mean supermarket chains, mass merchandisers such as Wal-Mart, Kmart and Target, and drugstores and warehouse clubs such as Costco and Sam's Club."[4]

Ralston Purina, the largest pet food manufacturer, made a decision in late 2001 to sell its pet food division to Swiss giant Nestlé for a reported $10.3 billion. The company is now known as Nestlé Purina Pet Care Center. (Previous purchases by Nestlé include Carnation in 1985, which owned Friskies. And in 1994, Nestlé had purchased the Alpo brand dog food.)

As a part of the sale, Nestlé agreed with the Federal Trade Commission (FTC) stipulation to sell Meow Mix and Alley Cat, (two dry foods made by Purina) to the Boston-based investment firm J.W. Childs Equity Partners ll L.P., which owns the pet supply company Hartz Mountain.[5]

"Ralston's share of the dry cat food market across all channels of distribution is approximately 34%," noted the FTC. "Nestlé has a market share of approximately 11% of the dry cat food market across all channels of distribution....Nestlé also adds Ralston's 28 percent share of the dog food market to the 10 percent it already has."[6] It is clear that this new company will control a vast percentage of the pet food market.

Pet Food Companies and Law Suits

Law suits within the pet food industry surfaced in 2001. According to the *Dayton Business Journal,* "Nutro Products and Kal Kan Food Inc.—rivals of pet food manufacturer Iams—have filed separate lawsuits in federal court during the past two months that question Iams' 55-year-old integrity and its marketing message that Iams dog food is 'good for life.'"[7]

In 1999, under new ownership, Iams began updating its feeding guidelines for Eukanuba and Iams dog foods. These guidelines suggested lowering the recommended amount of food to feed dogs each day. In their lawsuits, Nutro and Kal Kan, allege that this causes the dogs to lose weight in dangerous amounts. The suit claims that dogs fed according to Iams' instructions won't receive sufficient nutrition. "Iams executives deny that the feeding instructions are inappropriate and say the allegations in the lawsuits are without merit," reported Greg Johnson in an October 2001 article in the *Los Angeles Times.*[8]

It was not just Kal Kan and Nutro that initiated lawsuits claiming Iams engaged in a misleading marketing campaign that attempted to make the pricier Iams brand seem less expensive by reducing the recommended daily amounts of certain Iams foods. On March 5, 2001, the law firm of Wasserman, Comden & Casselman, L.L.P. filed a class action lawsuit in Los Angeles County Superior Court against the Iams Company and Procter and Gamble Company. "The complaint was filed on behalf of all persons who purchased Iams dog food products from April 1999 to the present," according to the lawyers.[9]

Basically, this class action lawsuit states that consumers were misled concerning the nutritional value of all Eukanuba and Iams brands of dog foods. "Five independent studies were conducted to test the statements made by Iams," states the report from the legal firm. "In all of the five studies, the humane officer terminated the testing early due to significant weight loss suffered by the dogs following Iams' feeding instruction."[10] The complaint was initially launched by Karen Pollack who had fed her dog, Ally, Iams Chunks and found that her dog had lost more than four pounds while following Iams' feeding guidelines.

Iams representatives claimed that they had decided in 1999 to lower the amount of food recommended for dogs because of evidence that obesity in dogs had become a national problem. However, according to studies based on Nutro Products' analysis, "The recommended feeding levels listed on Iams Chunks will support only the maintenance of an inactive dog. The label on the dog food, however, claims it is for normally active dogs."[11] It is apparent that either Iams changes the feeding instructions on its dog food or continues to be involved in a number of lawsuits initiated by other pet food companies or pet owners who have seen weight loss in their pets while feeding this product.

Pet Food Manufacturers and Veterinarians

We have all taken our pets to the veterinary clinic for one reason or another. Most clinics that I have visited have had the walls lined with various kinds of pet foods, some prescription, some nonprescription. In my opinion, this is unethical unless a veterinarian has training in pet nutrition. Our family physician doesn't display weight loss products in the reception room. Our family doctor doesn't sell food that may stop kidney disease or aid in the treatment of diabetes. So why is this going on in veterinary clinics that do not specialize in nutrition?

Most veterinarians acquire their only knowledge on pet nutrition in elective classes in veterinary school. These classes may only last a few weeks and are often taught by representatives from pet food companies. Hill's, Iams, and Purina are the largest contributors for these courses. In addition, pet food companies even donate food to the vet students for their own companion animals. This practice has become so widespread among pet food companies that the veterinary school at Colorado State University made this an agenda item for an Executive Committee meeting in 2000. "Discussion was held on how to handle dealing with pet food companies and their donations of pet food to the university," according to the Executive

Committee minutes. "It was agreed to put together a task force to discuss this issue, investigate the possibilities, and make suggestions to the Executive Council on how to work with the numerous pet food companies that want to donate to CSU."[12] Subsequent Executive Committee minutes make no further mention of this topic.

In a news release issued by Ralston Purina in May 2000, the pet food company announced that "in an effort to help university, veterinary hospitals provide optimal nutrition recommendations for dogs and cats, Ralston Purina is funding three new veterinary diet technician positions."[13] The company funded $100,000 to support three new diet technician positions for the first year. (The three schools benefiting from funding for veterinary diet technician positions were Texas A&M, University of Pennsylvania, and Virginia-Maryland Regional College of Veterinary Medicine.) Purina also states that they provide educational outreach activities at twenty-seven veterinary schools across the United States. Would it be safe to assume that these diet technicians, once graduated, would be promoting other pet foods?

Pet food manufacturers also make donations to veterinary schools in Canada. For example, the Iams Company donates both therapeutic and maintenance diets for feline and canine patients as well as other animals at the Ontario Veterinary College at Guelph.

In correspondence from a veterinarian who requested anonymity, she related her experiences while in veterinary school. "The pet food companies plied students with free pizza, free pet food, bags, binders, and even purses with the particular company's logo embossed on everything," according to the former veterinary student. Pet food companies also hire students to be reps in order to facilitate information dissemination on particular pet foods to the student body. This former veterinary student also noted that at no time was there ever a course offered on preparing a homemade diet for pets or its possible benefits. If you are lucky enough to have a veterinarian who is versed in how to prepare a homemade diet for your pet you can bet that he/she acquired this knowledge from independent studies.

Pet Food Manufacturers and Animal Organizations

In addition to their involvement with veterinary schools, pet food companies also make major donations to organizations related to animal companion interests. For example, in 1997 Hill's Science Diet pledged $1 million to the American Veterinary Medical Association (AVMA). "These funds will support the AVMA convention and a myriad of other meetings in disaster relief, animal welfare, educational symposia, and veterinary practice management,"[14] states Robert Wheeler, president and CEO of Hill's in a press release. He also notes how Hill's already supports the profession from scientific presentations at national veterinary meetings to furnishing diets to the thirty-one veterinary colleges and sixty-eight technology schools in the United States.

In February 2002 Hill's Science Diet signed a wide-ranging agreement with The Humane Society of the United States (HSUS). Hill's will be providing "generous financial support to several HSUS programs over the next few years."[15] Among the perks, Hill's will provide participating shelters with free food to feed all the dogs and cats at the shelter. In return, the shelter will purchase, at wholesale price, small bags of Science Diet to give each adopter at the time of adoption.

In addition, The HSUS noted that Hill's will provide $30,000 annually to be earmarked for scholarships, grants, or tuition reimbursements to staff or shelters participating in the Shelter Partners program. This money will allow individuals to attend various HSUS events, including Humane Society University, The HSUS Pets for Life National Training Center, and Animal Care Expo. Hill's will also be a sponsor of the Animal Care Expo and the lead sponsor of The HSUS Pets for Life National Training Center in Denver.[16]

Ralston Purina, another large contributor, is involved in providing funds and pet foods to the American Kennel Association. In 1999, Ralston Purina presented $71,260 to the American Kennel Club Canine Health Foundation. The donation came from two sources: A gift of $21,260 came from matching contributions received from Ralston Purina and the International Kennel Club (IKC) for adult-dog entries in the February 27, 1999 benched show. "Ralston Purina also donated $50,000 from contributions received from ticket sales for the Purina Charity Ball held on February 27 and the samples of Purina brand pet foods at the Purina booth at dog show events during the past year,"[17] states a press release by Purina. Some companies have ingenious ways to promote their products.

It continually amazes me how pet food companies promote their products, especially through the veterinary profession. Money, perks, and awards await anyone in the profession who is willing to promote these company products. Pharmaceutical companies used to run rampant with perks offered to medical doctors hoping to influence the use of their drugs. Fortunately, this practice has been widely curbed. My hope is that veterinary medicine and nonprofit animal organizations rethink their relationships with pet food companies.

– *Six* –

Mad Cow Disease
and Animal Companions

Mad cow disease, also called bovine spongiform encephalopathy (BSE), is a disease the general public often heard about in the 1990s as large numbers of cattle in the United Kingdom contracted it and died. In 1985 the first case of BSE was detected in the United Kingdom and by 1990 there were at least fifteen thousand confirmed cases of BSE in the country. By September 2001, BSE had infected 181,368 cattle in the United Kingdom and had spread to other countries, including Belgium, Denmark, France, Germany, Ireland, Italy, Japan, Netherlands, Portugal, Spain, and Switzerland.

There are many theories that exist on the causation of mad cow disease. The consensus among scientists is that the cattle had eaten feed contaminated with BSE. Apparently rendered material used to make cattle feed included the remains of sheep infected with scrapie (the sheep form of BSE). Although this rendered material had been fed to cattle for many years, BSE in cattle was virtually an unheard of disease until the mid-1980s. If this was the case, why was there a major breakout of BSE in the United Kingdom?

One plausible reason is that U.K. renderers lowered the temperatures in the rendering process in 1980. In addition, solvents, which had been used in the rendering process, were excluded. Experts studying the BSE epidemic surmised that up until the early 1980s the renderers in the United Kingdom used flammable solvents to dissolve fats and the solvents may have deactivated the agent that causes mad cow disease and scrapie. When the use of these solvents was discontinued this may have allowed the scrapie agent to remain viable. It was shortly after renderers stopped using these solvents that the first cases of BSE began to appear in cattle in the United Kingdom. Although this has been one of the theories posed, many other theories exist and an exact cause has never been established.

Scrapie and BSE are caused by a prion, which is neither a bacteria nor a virus. According to Stanley Prusiner, PhD, professor of neurology and biochemistry at the University of California and a 1997 Nobel Prize recipient in medicine, "Prions are an infectious protein without detectable DNA or RNA [Ribonucleic acid]."[1] It is believed that prions cannot be destroyed by cooking, freezing, ionizing, radiation, autoclaving, sterilization, bleach, or formaldehyde.

Some scientists theorize that the changes in the rendering process—lower temperatures and lack of solvents—may have contributed to the spread of BSE. The "BSE Inquiry," a group of doctors and scientists in the United Kingdom have other theories. This group of doctors noted that the most puzzling aspect was that only one or two cattle in a herd became infected with BSE even though the entire herd was fed the same compound. "The theory was that the rendering process might produce meat and bone meal that was not perfectly mixed and homogeneous," the BSE Inquiry committee concluded. "A small amount of BSE infective material might end up confined to a pocket or clump of meat and bone meal consumed by one or two cows, having not been broken down sufficiently during the rendering process to cause the BSE agent to spread evenly throughout the batch."[2]

This, along with the fact that there was an endemic amount of scrapie present in the United Kingdom at that time, could well have contributed to the spread of mad cow disease. In addition, cattle, who once grazed in pastures, were fed more rendered material that contained diseased sheep as well as diseased cattle. As the cattle died, they also were rendered and processed into livestock feed and into pet food.

Human Form of Mad Cow Disease

When people began eating cattle infected with BSE, the disease then jumped species to humans. The human form of BSE is called Creutzfeldt-Jakob Disease (CJD) and is always fatal. Although the British government assured consumers that eating beef was safe, in 1995 three people died from what is described as the new variant Creutzfeldt-Jakob Disease. This is called "new variant" because the age of the people dying includes teens and young adults in their twenties and early thirties. Prior to the 1995 outbreak there was only Sporadic CJD, which affects about one in a million people with an average age of sixty-seven. Sporadic CJD is not caused by the BSE agent, but occurs spontaneously and is always fatal.

As of September 2002, the U.K. Creutzfeldt-Jakob Disease Surveillance Unit in Edinburgh listed 115 cases of the new variant CJD in the United Kingdom and France. One case has been reported in the United States and another in Canada. Officials state that these two people in North America contracted the disease while residing in the United Kingdom at the height of the epidemic.

Steven Best, BA, PhD, from the University of Texas is concerned that CJD in the United States is seriously undiagnosed. He believes that CJD fatalities often are not recorded on death certificates since doctors tend to refuse autopsies of suspected CJD victims. In his report, "Cows, Cannibalism, Capitalism & Coverup," Dr. Best suggests, "It is easy to misdiagnose CJD as Alzheimer's disease, the fourth leading cause of death in the U.S., currently afflicting two to three million people."[3] Dr. Best cites 1989 autopsy studies done at the University of Pittsburgh and Yale University that show respectively that 5.5 percent and 13 percent of Alzheimer patients actually were victims of CJD.[4]

In a similar survey of neuropathologists it was found that from 2 percent to 12 percent of all dementias in humans were actually CJD. This survey finding was corroborated by a 1989 University of Pennsylvania study by Elias E. Manuelidis, MD, and Laura Manuelidis, MD, which identified that 5 percent of misdiagnosed dementia patients were actually dying from CJD.[5]

If these studies are accurate, what government action is being undertaken to see that the human meat supply is free from BSE? What steps are being taken by government agencies to insure that humans are not infected with CJD from eating contaminated meat? I can't help but wonder that if the U.S. and Canadian governments are so lax about the possibility of CJD and mad cow disease existing in North America and threatening human beings, how could they possibly care what might be in pet food?

Diseased Cats and Zoo Animals

Transmissible spongiform encephalopathies (TSEs) affect and kill a number of species. For example, BSE is a form of a TSE. All TSEs are caused by prions, including CJD.

Between 1990 and March 2002 nearly ninety house cats have died of the feline form of mad cow disease, which is called feline spongiform encephalopathy (FSE). The first cat identified as having FSE was a Siamese cat in the United Kingdom named Max who died in 1990. Some veterinarians suspect that many more cats have died since then, but these deaths have not been recorded because owners either do not have autopsies performed on their cats' brains or the cats wandered off to die alone. Autopsies are the only way to determine if a cat died from FSE.

Lukas Perler, DVM, from the Federal Veterinary Office in Bern, Switzerland stated, "The average incubation period in cats with feline spongiform encephalopathy (FSE)—the interval between the time of infection and the time of emergence of the disease symptoms—is about five years, which is comparable to BSE in cattle."[6]

According to the Neuro Center at the University of Bern in Switzerland, a reference laboratory for spongiform encephalophies in animals, "Affected cats show a lack of coordination with an ataxia mainly of the hind limbs, they often fall and miss their target when jumping. Fear and increased aggressiveness against the owner and also other animals is often seen.... Cats with FSE in general show severe behavioural disturbances, restlessness and depression, and a lack of coat cleaning."[7] The Neuro Center also notes that FSE-infected cats no longer tolerate touch (stroking), they start hiding, and they have excessive salivation.

As of March 2001, a number of zoo animals have died from TSEs. These include five cheetahs, six kudus, three lions, three ocelots, six eland, two ankole cows, one bison, one gemsbok, one nyala, one Arabian oryx, and one scimitar oryx, These animals were from zoos in the United Kingdom and Europe whose deaths are attributed to contaminated feed.[8]

In July 2002 a report from the Chief Veterinarian in Canberra, Australia, Gardner Murray, DVM, made a presumptive diagnosis for TSE on a male Asiatic golden cat in the Melbourne Zoo. This cat had been imported from a European zoo to the Melbourne Zoo in 1998. "Histopathological findings in this case included spongiform changes in the white matter tracts of various parts of the brain,"[9] wrote Dr. Murray. In the Melbourne Zoo the cat had been fed whole rabbits, chickens, rats, and kangaroo meat. He added, "As such it is virtually certain that exposure to TSE occurred at a time before the animal was imported into Australia."

Diseased Animals in Pet Food?

The FDA states that transmitting BSE to pets through pet foods in the United States is low because pet foods containing meat cannot be imported from at-risk countries such as the United Kingdom. In addition, all meat in U.S. pet foods comes from U.S. animals, and supposedly all U.S. meat sources are free of BSE.

In the past, other countries such as the United Kingdom, also claimed that their animals were free of BSE. If we are to believe that the United States and Canada are free from BSE, then we need to at least be concerned about other TSEs that do exist in both countries. The three sprongiform diseases that are presently in the United States and Canada are scrapie in sheep, TSE in mink, and chronic wasting disease in captive and wild herds of deer and elk.

Scrapie

Scrapie is the sheep form of a TSE. Most countries have some outbreaks of scrapie, including the United States. Only two countries are considered to be "scrapie free"—Australia and New Zealand.

Scrapie was first diagnosed in sheep in the United States in 1947. The symptoms of scrapie in sheep include an unsteady gait, itching, and behavioral changes that include nervousness, aggressive behavior, and isolation from the rest of the flock. From 1947 until July 2001 scrapie has been diagnosed in more than one thousand flocks of sheep. However, the USDA advises, "There is no epidemiological evidence that scrapie poses a risk to human health."[10] Perhaps not to human health but we do know that cattle and other animals who were fed the rendered remains of scrapie-infected sheep and BSE-infected cattle developed this brain-eating disease. How does the scenario differ in the United States?

First, the population of sheep in the United States is small compared to that in the United Kingdom. Second, in 1989 the American rendering industry initiated a voluntary program under which no sheep heads are to be accepted at rendering plants. This program was initiated when it became apparent that sheep infected with scrapie might be a source of the BSE outbreak in the United Kingdom, which had begun in 1985. However, the program was voluntary and not all U.S. rendering plants cooperated. According to *The New York Times*, "An Agriculture Department survey, three years later, found that 6 of 11 rendering plants inspected did accept sheep heads."[11]

In addition, the United States, like the United Kingdom, stopped using solvents as a regular part of the rendering process, which some scientists theorize could be related to the BSE outbreak in the United Kingdom. According to a report from the BSE Inquiry, "By 1970, most of the solvent extraction plants in the U.S. had blown up, burned down, or closed for safety."[12]

Basically, the United States was left wide open for a BSE outbreak. By 1985, renderers were still rendering sheep heads, solvents were no longer a part of U.S. rendering, and very few cattle were being tested for BSE. Other than the fact that the United States rendered far fewer sheep then the United Kingdom, it is possible that a different form of BSE might be infecting cattle in the United States. Richard Marsh, DVM, undertook some revealing tests that validate this possibility, as described in the following sections.

TSE in Mink

There are other prion diseases that have not affected human health; however, they are diseases in animals to watch carefully. One of those is transmissible spongiform encephalophathy (TSE) in mink , which was first detected in the United States in 1947. Since then, there have been twenty-five outbreaks of TSE in the United States that have killed tens of thousands of mink. This perplexed researchers because they had been unable to intentionally infect mink in the lab with TSE by feeding them scrapie-infected sheep brains.

A breakthrough in understanding TSE in mink came in 1985 when TSE wiped out more than seven thousand mink at a mink ranch in Wisconsin. These animals were fed almost exclusively on rendered dairy cows called "downers." Downers is the meat and dairy industry's term for factory farm animals who have fallen and died from "unexplainable causes."[13] (People in animal reform attribute the cause for downed livestock to the inhumane treatment of animals raised on factory farms and the stressful procedures when transporting the animals for slaughter.) Marc Lappé, PhD, works with Ethics and Toxics, a nonprofit environmental group based in California. He asserts that an estimated three hundred thousand farm animals who die each year are classified as "downers."

When University of Wisconsin veterinary scientist Richard Marsh inoculated U.S. cattle with the infected mink brains, the cattle died. When Dr. Marsh fed the brains of these cows to healthy mink, they also died of a TSE. Dr. Marsh theorized that an indigenous U.S. strain of BSE already existed and that it manifests itself as a "downer cow" disease rather than as "mad cow" disease as found in the United Kingdom.

When Dr. Marsh undertook these experiments in 1985, the prion theory was just that—a theory. Scientists had first identified prions in the 1970s, however, it was not until about 1987 that prions were connected to BSE or any of the TSE diseases. The British government, as well as all renderers internationally, assumed that rendering destroys this disease.

Who Disposed of the Diseased Animals?

Seven thousand mink died at this ranch in Wisconsin. How were they disposed of? The cattle injected with the infected mink brains also died. How were they disposed of? These are two important questions that apparently no one has delved into. The U.S. government continues to deny that this disease exists in the United States, but unless these mink and cattle were incinerated, it does exist.

My queries regarding how the diseased mink and cattle in the United States were disposed of began with the Food and Drug Administration/Center for Veterinary Medicine (FDA/CVM) in 1995. The questions I asked included, "Were these animals buried, incinerated, or rendered?" The FDA/CVM did not reply. My next letter was directed to Dr. Marsh, who had performed the mink-to-cattle experiments. Dr. Marsh never responded to my inquiries, and he died in March 1997. My final query was posed to another doctor with the FDA and as of November 2002, I have not received an answer on what happened to the diseased carcasses of these mink and cattle.

In early 1997, I contacted a person who works for the USDA (who has requested anonymity) on a matter unrelated to the mink and cattle situation. Realizing that this person might have knowledge in this area, I asked if he was aware of how the cattle and mink in Dr. Marsh's tests were disposed of. His reply was, "I'd have to check my references for the results of Marsh's work, but it is my understanding that the mink were rendered and fed back to other mink and the cattle involved in the research were similarly disposed of."[14] Were these cattle rendered and fed back to other cattle? According to the Physicians Committee for Responsible Medicine, one teaspoon of BSE-contaminated food can transmit the disease to other animals.

Chronic Wasting Disease

Another prion disease that people should be carefully tracking is Chronic Wasting Disease (CWD). CWD is found in deer and elk in the United States and Canada. CWD was first observed in elk at a research facility in Ft. Collins, Colorado in 1967. However, it was not until the late 1970s that CWD was recognized as a transmissible spongiform encephalopath (TSE). Since then, other cases have been found in deer and elk in Montana, Wyoming, South Dakota, Oklahoma, Nebraska, New Mexico, Wisconsin, and the province of Saskatchewan.

This disease has been found on ranches as well as in wild deer and elk. Symptoms for CWD include weight loss, behavioral changes, excessive salivation, increased thirst and urination, stumbling, and trembling, and finally death. Diagnosis of CWD is based on microscopic examination of brain and tonsil tissue.

According to the Western Association of Fish and Wildlife, "Neither the agent causing chronic wasting disease nor its mode of transmission have been definitively identified but clinical disease is associated with the accumulation of protease-resistant prion protein."[15] Experimental and circumstantial evidence suggests that the method of CWD transmission was through animal-to-animal contact and/or contamination of feed and water sources with saliva, urine, and/or feces.

It is still debatable if CWD can be spread to livestock or humans. Three hunters in the United States, ranging in age from early twenties to early thirties, have died of CJD disease. However, it has not been attributed to the new variant form of CJD, which is what happened when BSE broke loose in the United Kingdom. These hunters died of what is classified as the sporadic form of CJD, which occurs in about one in a million people. Government officials feel that *these* deaths were not caused by the hunters eating meat from the deer or elk they hunted, which might have had CWD. Instead, government officials maintain that the hunters died from a naturally occurring form of CJD.

Beth Williams, DVM, PhD, a leading expert on CWD, advises hunters "to wear latex or rubber gloves when dressing harvested deer or elk, and washing up afterwards; avoid contact with brain and spinal cord; discard the head, spine, spleen, and lymph nodes."[16]

Mad Cow Disease in the United States and Canada

In August 1997 the FDA issued a ban to prohibit the feeding of any mammalian protein to ruminant animals such as cows, sheep, and goats. This meant that rendered cattle, goats, deer, elk, or mink could not be used in any feed products for cattle. The FDA ruling did not rule out the use of protein derived from swine and equine sources. In addition, nothing was banned from use in pet foods, even though there were known cases of felines contracting TSEs in the United Kingdom, Northern Ireland, Norway, and Liechtenstein.

The FDA had also initiated the testing brains of cattle who might be suspect for BSE. The U.S. Department of Agriculture, Animal and Plant Health Inspection Services reported that from May 10, 1990 through December 31, 2001, the veterinary laboratories tested a total of 20,141 brains from cattle in the United States. This includes "neurologically ill cattle found on the farm. Neurologically ill cattle presented at veterinary diagnostic labs or hospitals. Rabies negative cattle. Cattle condemned at slaughter for neurological disease. Non-ambulatory (down/fallen stock.)"[17] All their tests proved negative for BSE.

The FDA claims that the United States is free from BSE. On the surface this would seem reassuring, however, the number of cattle brains tested for BSE is quite limited compared to the number of cattle slaughtered in any given time period. The Public Citizen, an organization that investigates problems within the government, notes, "In 2000, approximately 2,300 brains were tested out of 35 million cattle slaughtered."[18] This is indeed a small percentage tested of the total animals slaughtered.

As of July 2001 the National Agriculture Statistics Services estimated that there was a total of 105.8 million head of cattle and calves in the United States. It is apparent that a very small percentage of these animals are actually being tested. Food Animal Concern Trust (FACT) is an organization that promotes better methods of raising livestock and poultry. FACT's concerns are the age of cattle being slaughtered in the United States. FACT reports, "Scientists believe that cattle become infected with BSE usually between 1 and 2 years of age and that the disease has an incubation period of about 5 years. Beef cattle are customarily slaughtered at 18 months, when infection may occur but long before the disease becomes apparent. This early slaughter age may mask the existence of BSE in beef cattle across the nation."[19]

A number of nonprofit organizations, including the Public Citizen, Farm Sanctuary, and Organic Consumers Association, believe that the United States is leaving itself wide open for a BSE epidemic. Academics such as Steven Best, PhD, Associate Professor of Philosophy and Humanities at the University of Texas, and Michael Greger, MD, agree with this assessment. According to an article in *The Wall Street Journal,* there should be concern over the animal protein that has been imported from the United Kingdom into the United States between 1998 and December 2000. It was not until December 2000 that the USDA banned all imports of rendered animal proteins from thirty-one countries that either had BSE or presented an undue risk of introducing BSE into the United States.

The Wall Street Journal tracked how much animal protein came into the United States from those thirty-one countries. "The records, gleaned from U.S. Customs data, showed at least 72 shipments, including mammal-based bone meal, dried meat scraps, animal waste and blood," reported *The Wall Street Journal* in November 2001. "The countries included Belgium as well as places such as France, Germany, Italy, Spain and Japan, where mad-cow cases are on the rise."[20] *The Wall Street Journal* also stated that the FDA confirmed that thirty shipments of animal by-products had arrived in the United States after the ban took effect. Eleven of these shipments were tracked but the whereabouts of the other nineteen is unknown.

At the height of the U.K. mad cow epidemic, from 1993 to 1996, the United Kingdom exported 125 tons of meat and bone meal to Canada but so far the Canadian government advises that Canada is free of BSE. *The Sunday Times* in the United Kingdom reported that fifteen thousand tons of meat and bone meal were exported to France between 1988 and 1990. In February 1991 France saw its first case of BSE. As of December 2001, France has reported a total of 258 BSE cases and the disease is on the rise. Another country using meat and bone meal exported from the United Kingdom from 1989 through 1996 was the Netherlands. As of January 2002 the Netherlands reported thirty cases of BSE.

In addition, the United Kingdom exported twenty tons of suspect meal and bone meal to the United States in 1989 but no cases of mad cow disease have been reported or detected in the United States. Dr. Best believes that perhaps cattle in the United States may display a different strain of BSE. In Dr. Best's 1999 paper on BSE, he asserts, "If this is the case, then a BSE epidemic in the U.S. might not take the form of 'mad' cows staggering around with spongy holes in their brains, but rather 'downer' cows that simply collapse and die." [21]

According to the USDA's Animal and Plant Health Inspection Services, the American Association of Bovine Practitioners estimates that 195,000 American cattle succumb to downer-cow syndrome every year, and they are recycled into feed for hogs, chickens, pets, or directly routed to the human dinner plate. Because the United States purports to be BSE-free, the government believes that their testing methods are adequate to insure that all cattle going to slaughter are healthy.

Mad Cow Disease in Germany

Germany had long proclaimed it was BSE-free. It used the same testing on cattle that the United States has used for many years and continues to use. Meat inspectors, suspecting an animal has neurological disease, sends the head (brains) of that animal to a lab for BSE testing.

In the mid-1990s, Markus Moser, a PhD in molecular biology, who heads a Swiss company, Prionics, developed a rapid response test for BSE called the "Prionics Check Test." Moser says the test has found cases of mad cow disease in healthy cattle who would otherwise have entered the human food chain.

Prionics began marketing their rapid test detection to labs in Germany. Private labs performed the Prionics test on a small number of cattle and found BSE in German cows for the first time. "It snowballed from there," Jeffery Nelson reported in his article, "USDA Mad Cow Strategy," for *Veg Source*. "Germany did more rapid testing and found it had a big problem."[22] Up until the time Prionics developed the BSE test, Germany had reported only six cases of mad cow identified among cows imported from the United Kingdom between 1992 and 1999. But with the new BSE test, the numbers sky rocketed between 2000 and 2002. Germany has detected 147 cases of mad cow disease using the Prionics Check Test.

Detecting and Reporting Mad Cow Disease in the United States

Given the situation in Germany, the question begs to be asked: Are the United States and Canada doing an adequate job in insure that BSE is not in these countries? In my opinion, no!

Both countries are still using the old detection method of sending the brains of suspect cattle to veterinary labs. (The main lab, the National Veterinary Services Laboratories, is located in Ames, Iowa.) According to Arthur Davis, Chief of the Pathobiology Laboratory, "Minimum time after collection of the specimen for results would be 8 days."[23] When Jeffery Nelson from *Veg Source* questioned the legitimacy of the old detection method, Linda Detwiler, who chairs the BSE Working Group at the U.S. Department of Agriculture, defended current U.S. testing, asserting "it is adequate to detect mad cow if it is in the U.S."[24]

The result of using the older and more cumbersome method for BSE testing is that fewer cattle are tested in both countries as compared to the numbers tested in European countries. The statistics for testing cattle going to slaughter are alarmingly low in the United States compared to other countries. Consider the following: At present, the United States tests one out of every eighteen thousand cows slaughtered. In Germany, one out of every three healthy cattle slaughtered are tested. Switzerland tests one out of every sixty cows.

In September 2002, I contacted the Prionics company in Switzerland and asked if the United States and Canada planned to use the Prionics Check Test. Peter Mueller, a company representative, replied to my inquiry stating, "No decision was so far made by the American authorities concerning a BSE surveillance program using rapid diagnostic kits."[25] He went on to write that they are in constant contact with the American as well as the Canadian authorities, but it is apparent that a decision will not be made in the foreseeable future. Given the situation in Germany and other countries now using the Prionics test for early detection of BSE, I can only wonder why the United States and Canada are dragging their feet on approving this test for BSE detection of cattle.

The judgment of meat inspectors is highly problematic. Dr. Moser warns that the United States's method of relying on the inspectors in slaughterhouses to detect BSE is unreliable at best. "If a vet is not well educated in spotting signs of BSE, they [meat inspectors] can easily miss them."[26]

A Flawed Detection System in the United States

Given all that I have learned about BSE, its symptoms, and the devastating effect it can have on the cattle industry, I have to ask myself: *Does anyone really think if a farmer or veterinarian actually observed cattle displaying odd behavior that they would report this to the proper authorities?* I think not. They would be well aware of the consequences of their actions, and could quickly be made the scapegoats in bringing down a multi-billion dollar industry.

The 1997 ban in the United States on feeding meat and bone meal to cattle, sheep, and goats is extremely flawed. The Associated Press reported in March 2001 that "397 feed mills that are licensed by the FDA and also process meat and bone meal have no system for preventing those products from being mixed with other ingredients." The same article also reported that 15 percent of the feed mills were not using required warning labels. "There are 1,829 unlicensed feed mills that handle meat and bone meat, and a third of them did not comply with the labeling requirements. In addition, eighteen percent did not have systems to prevent mixups in feed ingredients."[27]

Many cats have died from the feline form of BSE in Europe after eating contaminated pet food. No cases of FSE have been documented in cats in the United States or Canada. Yet, I question how many veterinarians are actually aware of FSE and what symptoms to look for.

Cattle—dead, diseased, dying and disabled (4-D)—can legally be rendered and used in pet foods in the United States and in Canada. Rendering will not eradicate any of the TSEs, including the chronic wasting disease in deer, elk, and roadkill, which can also be rendered for use in pet food.

In 1997 Oprah Winfrey was sued by cattle ranchers because of a show she hosted in which her guests discussed beef and mad cow disease. The plaintiffs alleged that Winfrey wrongfully disparaged the U.S. beef industry, which negatively impacted their beef sales. In late 2000, while reading transcripts from the well-publicized trial, I noted that one of the plaintiffs, Paul Engler of Cactus Feeders, Inc., stated that "more than 10 cows with some sort of nervous system disorder were sent to Hereford By-Products."[28] Hereford By-Products is owned by Garth Merrick who also owns Merrick Pet Foods situated at the same location as the rendering plant. While reading this, it looked highly suspicious to me, and I wondered, *Were these cattle tested prior to being rendered?* Finding an answer to that question led me on a wild goose chase that forced me to turn to the Freedom of Information Act (FOIA).

First I inquired at the National Veterinary Services in Ames, Iowa, a lab that undertakes most of the testing of suspect cattle. I did not receive any information, and was referred to various government offices. Eventually, I filed a request for this information under the FOIA and waited eleven months for the reply. When the information arrived, the FOIA report stated, "Agency employees conducted a thorough search of their files but did not locate any records responsive to your request."[29]

Despite the government advising the public that testing is undertaken on cattle displaying symptoms of neurological disease, apparently it does not apply to all cattle. Perhaps one or two cattle displaying symptoms of neurological disease might be overlooked—but there were ten cows that displayed some sort of "central nervous system disorder" all at the same location and none of them were tested for BSE.

Conclusion

The U.S. government believes it is safe to render diseased cattle for use in pet foods because this practice does not affect humans since we don't eat dogs and cats. But rendering diseased cattle into pet food does potentially endanger our animal companions. This is already happening in Europe. If dogs and cats succumb to a TSE disease, would their owners know the actual cause?

Although cats have died from the feline form of this disease, no cases in dogs have been reported. When I asked Scott McEwen, DVM, at the Veterinary College, University of Guelph in Ontario, Canada, if neurological disease in dogs could be misdiagnosed and in fact could be a canine form of BSE, he replied, "It is technically impractical to examine the entire brain histologically. Obviously, if the disease has not been described in dogs, the location of lesions in the brain of a dog is also unknown."[30]

Should we worry about contamination in pet food? Julie Ingwersen, a reporter for Reuters wire service, quotes Stephen Payne, a spokesman for the Pet Food Institute, as saying, "The meat and bone meal produced in the United States remains an excellent source of protein and minerals for pets."[31]

Unfortunately, labels on pet food give no indication of the source for the meat and bone meal. Based on my past experience with most commercial pet food companies, I am not willing to blindly trust the well-being of my animal companions to a spokesperson from the pet food industry. Remember that although this material—meat meal, and meat and bone meal—can no longer be used in feed for cattle, it can still be used in commercial pet foods.

SEVEN

Animal Experimentation
and Pet Food Companies

Throughout the United States, Canada, the United Kingdom and many other countries, university laboratories are undertaking experiments on live dogs and cats for a variety of reasons. Many of these experiments are done in complete secrecy to prevent animal rights activists from protesting. However, since 1992 when the federal government passed a law making acts of vandalism in research clinics a federal offense, there has been a decrease in protests by demonstrators such as those with the Animal Liberation Front.

Animal research continues and although people protest, still thousands of animals are killed in the name of research every year. The Center for Laboratory Animal Welfare states that there are an estimated four million animals per year who are used to test the safety of cosmetics, food additives, packing materials, industrial chemicals, and fabric treatments, as well as drugs and vaccines. "This represents about 13 percent of all animals used in U.S. laboratories today," according to the Center for Laboratory Animal Welfare. "The other 87 percent are used in education and in basic biomedical research, including the development of new drugs and vaccines."[1] About 95 percent of the four million animals used in testing are mice, rats, and other rodents such as guinea pigs and hamsters. But rabbits, dogs, cats, primates, birds, and fish are also used.

Many of these animals are used in human medical research. Medical schools often use dogs to teach basic physiology and pharmacology. Nancy Harrison, MD, from the association, Doctors Against Dog Labs, writes, "In dog labs, students or instructors typically anesthetize a dog, cut open the dog's chest and use its beating heart to demonstrate principles of physiology and pharmacology. At the end of the demonstration, they kill the dog."[2] Dr. Harrison explains, "Like other concerned physicians, I am working to persuade the medical school I care most about—in my case University of California, San Diego (UCSD) where I did my residency in pathology—to develop alternatives to dog labs for teaching physiology and pharmacology."

In June 2002, The Humane Society of the United States (The HSUS), reported on the abuse by a veterinarian, Michael Podell, at Ohio State University, who was departing from his duties as a researcher at the university. Podell was to investigate whether methamphetamines stimulate the replication of feline immunodeficiency virus (FIV), a disease that some scientists believe bears some resemblance to human immunodeficiency virus (HIV) in humans. "Podell was the lead researcher on a five-year, $1.68 million study, funded by National Institute of Health (NIH), that infected cats with FIV, dosed them with methamphetamines [commonly known as speed], tested them, and finally euthanized and dissected them,"[3] reports The HSUS. Since his research was launched in late 2000, Podell and his researchers had infected more then one hundred felines. Critics of this study dismissed his findings stating FIV and HIV are two radically different viruses.

In correspondence with a woman who works in one of these labs at the University of Illinois, I asked if many animals are used in these experiments. "There are thousands of animals on campus," she replied. She described one experiment where researchers broke a limb on each of twenty-four dogs, then treated the dogs' broken limbs, and then euthanized them in order to study the effect of the treatment on the bone.

A number of university research facilities are carrying out experiments on dogs and cats that are funded by the pet food industry. Pet food companies defend these experiments as "necessary" in order to find out if certain ingredients (usually cheap ingredients) have an effect on the animals. Documented animal experimentation by some pet food companies include surgery, intentionally breaking bones, starvation, forced obesity, deprivation of key nutrients and minerals, induced kidney failure, intentional wounding, and surgical removal of parts of kidneys, livers, intestines, and stomachs. Animals are also killed in order to examine the bodies after an experiment.

Animal experimentation can cause untold pain and suffering. Yet, according to the pet food companies, all of this experimentation is in the name of science to improve the health of our animal companions.

Iams and Animal Experimentation

One pet food company in particular, Iams, has attracted a lot of negative publicity in the last few years because of the research the company has undertaken. *The Sunday Express,* a British newspaper, reported on these atrocities in May 2001, "Our investigation has revealed that hundreds of animals suffered incredible agony in experiments designed to perfect Iams. A huge dossier of research papers exposes how scientists deliberately induced kidney failure and other conditions in dogs and cats. Some experiments involved performing operations on healthy animals that were later killed."[4]

Some of the animal experiments were outlined by two animal rights organizations, In Defense of Animals, based in the United States, and Uncaged Campaigns, based in the United Kingdom. Iams claimed that it used these studies to support its nutritional claims, which it uses to market its products. Iams experimentation conducted on dogs and cats included:

- Twenty-eight cats' bellies were cut to see the effect of feeding them fiber, then the cats were killed. Bueno, AR, et al, *Nutrition Research,* Vol. 20, No. 9, pp. 1319-1328, 2000.
- Twenty-four young dogs were intentionally put into kidney failure; subjected to invasive experimentation, then killed. University of Georgia and the Iams Company, White, JV, et al, *American Journal of Veterinary Research,* Vol. 52, No. 8, pp. 1357-1365, 1991.

- Thirty-one dogs' kidneys were removed to increase the risk of kidney disease, then they were killed and dissected. University of Georgia and the Iams Company, Finco, DR, et al, *American Journal of Veterinary Research,* Vol. 55, No. 9, pp. 1282-1290, 1994.
- Bones in eighteen dogs' front and back legs were cut out and stressed until they broke, University of Wisconsin and the Iams Company, Crenshaw, TD, et al, Proceedings of 1998 Iams Nutrition Symposium.
- Ten dogs killed to study the effect of fiber in diets, Mississippi State University and the Iams Company, Buddington, RK, et al, *American Journal of Veterinary Research,* Vol. 60, No. 3, pp. 354-358, 1999.
- Eighteen male puppies' kidneys were chemically damaged; experimental diets were fed; tubes were inserted in their penises, then the puppies were killed, Colorado State University and the Iams Company, Grauer, GF, et al, *American Journal of Veterinary Research,* Vol. 57, No. 6, pp. 948-956, 1996.
- Twenty-eight cats surgically forced into kidney failure and either died during the experiment or killed to study the effects of protein, University of Georgia and the Iams Company, Proceedings of the 1998 Iams Nutrition Symposium.
- Fifteen dogs' bellies cut open; tubes attached to their intestines, the contents of which were pumped out every ten minutes for two hours, then the dogs were killed, University of Nebraska-Lincoln and the Iams Company, Hallman, JE, et al, *Nutrition Research,* Vol. 16, No. 2, pp. 303-313, 1996.
- Sixteen dogs' bellies cut open and parts of their intestines taken, University of Alberta and the Iams Company, *Journal of the American Society of Nutritional Sciences,* 1998.

- Healthy puppies, chicks, and rats had bone and cartilage removed to study bone and joint development, Purdue University and the Iams Company, Proceedings of the 2000 Iams Nutrition Symposium.
- Invasive procedures used to study bacteria in sixteen dogs' intestines, Texas A&M University and the Iams Company, Willard MD, et al, *American Journal of Veterinary Research,* Vol. 55, No. 5, May 1994.
- Twenty-four cats had their female organs and parts of their livers removed; were made obese, then were starved, University of Kentucky and the Iams Company, Ibrahim, WH, et al, *American Journal of Veterinary Research,* Vol. 61, No. 5, May 2000.
- Fifty-six dogs had their female organs removed to study beta carotene, Washington State University and the Iams Company, Weng, BC, et al, *Journal of Animal Science,* 78, pp. 1284-1290, 2000.
- Sixteen dogs' bellies repeatedly cut to take parts of their intestines, Texas A&M and the Iams Company, Willard, MD, et al, *Journal of the Veterinary Medical Association,* 8, pp. 1201-1206, 1994.
- Six dogs had tubes implanted into their intestines and fluid drained repeatedly to study cereal flours, University of Illinois and the Iams Company, Murray, SM, et al, *Journal of Animal Science,* 77, pp. 2180-2186, 1999.
- Thirty dogs intentionally wounded and patches of skin containing the wounds removed to study wound healing, Auburn University and the Iams Company, Mooney, MA, et al, *American Journal of Veterinary Research,* Vol. 59, No. 7, pp. 859-863, 1998.
- Five dogs' bellies cut open and tubes inserted into their intestines to study the effect of fiber, University of Illinois and the Iams Company, Muir, HE, et al, *Journal of Animal Science,* Vol. 74, pp. 1641-1648, 1996.

- Parts of twenty-eight dogs' large intestines removed to study the effects of fiber, University of Missouri and the Iams Company, Howard, MD, et al, *Journal of Animal Science*, Vol. 75 (Suppl. 1), pp. 136, 1997.
- Parts of sixteen dogs' intestines and immune system cut out to study the effects of fiber, University of Alberta and the Iams Company, Proceedings of the 1998 Iams Nutrition Symposium.
- Five dogs had tissue from large and small intestines removed to study intestinal tract needs, University of Illinois and the Iams Company, Proceedings of the 1998 Iams Nutrition Symposium.[5]

Procter and Gamble (P&G) purchased Iams in September 1999 and issued a code of ethics. Animal People, an on-line organization devoted to the health and welfare of pets, reported in June 2001 that P&G stated its intention to phase out animal testing as fast as alternatives can be developed and approved by regulators. According to P&G, "The new code of ethics reflects the decision made two years ago by Iams to start no further studies which required euthanasia of cats and dogs. It applies to all Iams research in the development of pet food, regardless of whether it is conducted by universities, our own scientists, or others."[6]

In its report, "Iams—The Suffering Behind the Science," Uncaged Campaigns reported, "Dr. Dan Cary, Director of Technical Communications for Iams said that his company cared about the welfare of animals. He justified the scientific studies as being carried out to save pets from illnesses and improve physical well-being."[7] This is hard to believe in light of one of their "scientific" studies. This study involved regularly inflicting chest wounds on twelve huskies, twelve poodles, and twelve Labradors to see if diet could affect fur regrowth.

Although P&G has stated that the company will phase out animal testing, this does not cover the testing done by outside laboratories. P&G claims it has no way of knowing exactly how many animals these outside labs might use in various experiments for the company. P&G contracts out animal research to various labs when the company does not have enough technicians available. Outside labs "would only report to us the number (animals) used in a final protocol," states Katherine Stitzel, Associate Director at P&G, also claiming that P&G would not know how these tests were conducted.[8]

Animal Experimentation in the Pet Food Industry

Be assured that Iams is not the only pet food company that undertakes animal experimentation. According to the Animal Protection Institute (API), based in California, "Other large pet food manufacturers, including Hill's, Waltham's, and Ralston Purina among others, have funded, sponsored or conducted many studies that caused significant pain, discomfort or distress, used invasive procedures and/or resulted in the death of the subject animals."[9] The British Union for the Abolition of Vivisection has uncovered alarming evidence of animal testing by pet food manufacturers not only in the United States but internationally.

In research funded by Alpo Pet Foods, USA, "9 dogs had their stomachs opened up and a tube sewn in connecting the small intestines with the outside of the body. The tubes were in place for on average 26 weeks during which a number of complications occurred, including post-operative wound infections, leaking of caustic gut effluent causing ulceration, inflammation and abscesses," writes the British Union for the Abolition of Vivisection.[10]

In another experiment funded by Alpo Pet Foods, USA, "15 cats, fed until obese, were then starved by only being given completely unpalatable food [called 'voluntary starvation' by researchers]. They lost 26-40% of their body weight and developed severe muscle wasting, dehydration, lethargy, major blood abnormalities and swollen and damaged livers. When finally given normal food, 11 were unable to eat and had to be tube-fed," reported the British Union for the Abolition of Vivisection.[11]

This organization also cites experiments carried out at Hill's Pet Nutrition, USA, "42 puppies fed a zinc depleted diet for 2 weeks suffered deficiency symptoms such as crushed plaques on their face and feet, lethargy and anorexia. In a further test, 5 out of one group of six puppies kept on zinc-free diet had to be removed from the test, as their symptoms were so severe. At the end of the test, dew claws, one canine tooth and testes were removed [surgically] from all puppies for zinc analysis."[12]

Lawrence Carter-Long from the Animal Protection Institute (API) also reports that pet food companies, Hill's, Waltham's, and Ralston Purina, among others, have funded, sponsored, or conducted many studies that caused pain and suffering and/or resulted in death of the animals. He cites one experiment where "18 dogs were killed so their bones could be harvested for research on bone strength."[13]

The Executive Director of API, Alan Berger, has lobbied for the pet food industry to adopt stringent guidelines for future research in order to prevent the needless suffering of animals. "While such guidelines would not be necessarily binding to manufacturers, they would set a reasonable standard for ethical, humane research and hopefully put an end to what can only be considered a disgraceful contradiction," stated Berger.[14]

Jean Hofve, DVM, presented these API guidelines at AAFCO's 91st annual convention in August 2001. Some of API's suggestions included:

- Prohibit experiments on healthy animals that would cause distress, discomfort, pain, injury, illness, disease, or death.
- Prohibit experiments on healthy animals that require the death of any animal in order to complete a study, e.g., for necropsy, histopathology, or any other type of post-mortem examination or evaluation.
- Eliminate invasive procedures during research and development of diets.
- Specific research on the relationship of nutrition and disease shall be limited to clinical studies; i.e., conducted on animals who are enrolled in the study by their guardians, who suffer from the disease(s) being studied, and who are not subjected to invasive procedures that will not directly benefit the animal and the study.

The final suggestion for the proposed guidelines revolved around feeding tests or feeding trials such as manufacturer's colony animals that, according to AAFCO, are considered acceptable. These animals should not be deprived of calories or nutrients that could result in discomfort, distress, pain, or illness.

University Animal Experimentation Funded by Pet Food Companies

In January 2002 I received an email from a student at the University of Illinois, Danielle Marino. Her concerns involved animal experiments being undertaken in the lab where she had previously worked. One particular study involved nine dogs being studied for nutritional research purposes. This program had been funded for the last ten years by Iams but was now funded by the United Soybean Board and a Belgium company, Tiense Suikerraffinaderiy N.V. (The Iams' study was finished but the Belgium company used the same dogs for its ongoing study.)

Marino described experimentation where the dogs have a cannula (a long thin tube that transfers liquids or solutions) implanted in their sides so samples of digested food can be taken. She advised me that in a phone call to the researcher questioning the necessity of this experiment, he informed Marino that he was not to blame for these studies. He undertakes this research because pet owners want dogs who defecate infrequently but still have healthy colons, so he fulfills this demand.

The dogs involved in this study were purchased as puppies from an operation that has been cited countless times for animal neglect. Now, the dogs are housed in the windowless basement of the Edward Madigan Lab at the University of Illinois and do not even have minimal comforts such as bedding and little interaction with other dogs or humans.

Marino reported the abuse to the Association of Veterinarians for Animal Rights (AVAR). Paula Kislak, DVM, with AVAR, reviewed the medical reports and the progress of the specific research animals and additional research on the subject.

Dr. Kislak concluded: "Illegal cannulization is an unnecessary invasion surgical procedure that may even compromise the study's results due to potential chronic low-grade leakage, infection, irritation, and possible need for antibiotics, all of which alter intestinal microflora."[15] Dr. Kislak maintains that useful and adequate information could be obtained by analyzing the fecal material alone, and any animal experimentation or surgical interventions are not necessary.

In communications with Marino in February 2002, she reported that basically nothing had changed at the lab, but that she and a group of students continue to lobby for more humane treatment of these dogs. Marino also stated that these are not the only animals who are being used in research at the University of Illinois.

Dan Lyons, Director of Uncaged Campaigns, aptly summoned up my feelings when he wrote, "No reasonable person can ever accept the conduct of painful and lethal experiments on one animal in the distant hope that some information might emerge that might be useful for another animal. After all, this is similar to what the Nazis did—experiment on some humans supposedly to try to benefit other humans."[16]

Iams Creates an Award in Memory of a Vivisector

In January 2002, In Defense of Animals, an organization devoted to ending the exploitation and abuse of animals, issued a press release announcing that Iams was sponsoring a new award for "Achievements in Animal Biology." In Defense of Animals emphasized that this award was named for James E. Corbin, PhD, "a vivisector at the University of Illinois who spent fifty years conducting painful and lethal experiments on animals to develop commercial pet foods."[17]

Some of the experiments credited to Dr. Corbin include force-feeding dogs, which resulted in muscle tremors, vomiting, and frothing around the mouth. Twenty-four female beagle dogs were overfed and starved respectively to estimate body fat. All the dogs were eventually killed and their bodies were drained of blood and passed through a carcass grinder. In another experiment credited to Dr. Corbin, sixteen kittens were fed a deficient diet resulting in eye damage. The researchers punctured the hearts, drew blood, and then gassed the kittens. These are just a few of Dr. Corbin's experiments outlined by In Defense of Animals.

Pet food companies are honoring people like this? Honoring people who have caused pain and suffering to animals? This is what pet food companies rationalize as necessary in the name of science and a better pet food for our cats and dogs?

– *EIGHT*–

Homecooked Meals and Natural Pet Food Companies

R
epeatedly, the pet food industry and many veterinarians warn pet owners that human food should never be fed to cats and dogs. However, since 1990 I have encountered wonderful veterinarians who recommend that we avoid commercial foods and opt for a homemade diet. Drs. Wendell Belfield, Shawn Messonnier, Richard Pitcairn, Alfred Plechner, and Martin Goldstein are among those leading veterinarians speaking out on this topic and writing books. (Several of these books are noted in the Resource Section.) A growing number of veterinarians believe that pets enjoy a much healthier and longer life if we take the time to cook for them. Dr. Belfield states in his book, *How to Have a Healthier Dog,* "What's wrong with carrots and peas and salad and even fruits and cooked cereal? Nothing that I know of. I know a retired veterinarian in his eighties who has been feeding generations of dogs from table scraps. Meat, vegetables, grains, fruit."[1]

In the mid-1970s pet food began to imitate human food in appearance: Pet food burgers that resemble real hamburger, meat-balls in gravy (a concoction described as stew), and the latest, pasta. These humanized foods are designed to appeal to owners more than the pet with the help of additives such as dyes, flavor enhancers, humectants, texturizers, and emulsifiers. Synthetic preservatives approved for use in commercial pet food include butylated hydroxyanisole (BHA) and butylated hydroxytoluene (BHT), propyl gallate, propylene glycol, and ethoxyquin. There is little information available on the toxicity, interactions, or the effect these additives might have on pets who are ingesting them on a daily basis. Quite honestly, human food is barraged with numerous additives as well, and many of these are highly questionable regarding their long-term effects on our health.

Some pet food companies, primarily the ones selling "natural" foods, are using natural substances to preserve their products—vitamins C, E, and rosemary are the most common. Pet foods preserved naturally do not have an extended shelf-life like most commercial pet foods doused in chemical preservatives; however, they are a much safer food to feed your animal companions.

However, if you are not able or willing to cook for your animal companions, add some whole foods to their diet. Leftover meat or vegetables from your own meals are a good choice but avoid giving them junk food or highly seasoned foods. Carrots, celery sticks and apple slices are wholesome, easy treats to have on hand. Whole grain crackers are a favorite of my guys—both the dog and the cats. If you can combine some fresh snacks and family leftovers, along with a pet food that uses human grade ingredients, your animal companion should be eating well!

All-Natural Pet Food Companies

Over the years many readers have asked if there are commercial foods that I might consider feeding my animal companions because, as most readers know, I cook for my dog and cats. Some of the companies that I have researched and that seem to produce healthy pet food as of 2002, include the following list. Note that this list may not be complete, and I always welcome additional information on other high-quality pet foods that are composed of human-grade ingredients.

Halo, Purely for Pets is based in Palm Harbor, Florida, and prides itself in producing pet food that is of human-grade quality and made in USDA-approved kitchens. I have fed my animal companions Spot's Stew, and they were quite pleased. The only minor problem was that my cats found the green beans a little too large, which I quickly remedied by mashing them with a fork. Andi Brown, the owner of Halo, Purely for Pets, announced that the company has launched a new pureed formula for cats, which contains chicken and clams.

K9 Gourmet, based in Vancouver, British Columbia, was started in 1997 by Tracy Turnell when she began cooking for her dog. Since then the company has grown from Tracy cooking for her own dog and friends' dogs to a company that is now supplying pet stores, health food stores, and veterinary clinics in British Columbia, Washington, and Oregon. The company produces two lines of dog food, chicken and beef formula, and lamb and rice formula. K9 Gourmet is baked at moderate temperatures and frozen fresh from the oven. K9 Gourmet only uses human grade ingredients and there are no chemical additives, by-products. preservatives, dyes, salt, or sugar.

Natura Pet Products was founded by John and Ann Rademakers and Peter Atkins in Santa Clara, California. It produces a line of dry and canned foods for dogs and cats. They use only human-grade food, and their bottomline is, "If I wouldn't eat it, why would I want to feed it to my pet?" There are no artificial preservatives, colors or additives, and they pay attention to quality control. This is another food that I have fed my pets. Because my German shepherd, Sarge, was a little overweight and also had dry skin, we chose to feed the Lite Lamb and Rice formula. This did seem to solve his dry skin problem and the food contains few ingredients that might cause allergies. My cats, being rather fussy eaters, refused to eat the Innova dry food and also the Innova lite canned food, but they did enjoy the Innova cat food, which seems to have a better consistency for cats.

Canidae Pet Foods is a company based in San Luis Obispo, California. This company produces Canidae for dogs and Felidae for cats. The pet food contains only human-grade ingredients naturally preserved along with probiotics, digestive enzymes, herbs, antioxidants, amino acids, and amino acid chelated minerals. This food includes ten skin and coat conditioners with balanced omega-6 and omega-3 fatty acids. The Felidae includes cranberries for a healthy urinary tract. This product does not contain corn, wheat, soy, grain, or other fillers.

Old Mother Hubbard is located in Lowell, Massachusetts, started in 1926, and purchased in 1961 by Jim Scott, a professional animal nutritionist. This company makes Wellness, a baked natural pet food that does not contain animal by-products, wheat, corn, soybean, eggs, animal fat, or dairy products—all of which may cause allergies in dogs and cats. Deboned chicken, ocean whitefish, ground whole barley, sweet potatoes, and carrots are the main ingredients in Wellness. Cranberries and blueberries are added to the cat food to provide proper urinary tract health.

PetGuard, located in Florida, has been in business since 1979. This company uses only natural and certified organic ingredients, including human grade beef, pesticide free grains, and natural preservatives. All minerals used in this food are chelated, which increases the bioavailability (allowing more minerals to be absorbed into the system). There are no by-products, fillers, artificial colors, or preservatives. This company also encourages a "natural approach," which means occasionally adding portions of fresh meat and vegetables to a pet's diet.

Homemade Diets for Pets

Many people have told me that they are terrified that if they feed their pet anything other than what comes out of a can or bag they may be harming their beloved animals. They believe that their pet will keel over and die. If your animal companion has a serious health problem, first consult a holistic or naturopathic veterinarian. Then try feeding your pet a homemade diet.

I have attempted to provide a diet for my pets that incorporates all the protein, carbohydrates, fiber, and fats that they require. Much controversy revolves around the cooking and not cooking of the protein matter. Because I have researched all aspects of the meat industry, including conditions at some slaughterhouses, I *always* cook the meat for my guys. In cooking the meat, some of the healthy enzymes are destroyed, but so are the harmful bacteria and parasites.

Many pet owners have asked me about a raw meat and bone diet versus a cooked diet for cats and dogs. In my second book, *Protect Your Pet: More Shocking Facts,* I share the findings from my extensive research. I conclude that this is not a safe diet to feed companion animals, and there is no sound scientific information to confirm this assertion. Not only are dogs and cats as prone to the many bacteria in meat—Salmonella, Campylobactor, E. coli, and Listeria—as are humans, but some of these agents can be transmitted to the humans preparing the raw meat diet.

There are also tremendous problems with animal companions ingesting bones. I have read many sad stories by pet owners about the deaths of their animal companions after eating bones and succumbing to the bacteria in raw meat. One letter described a terrier, who, after vomiting, collapsed on his side in a pool of thick, bloody diarrhea. Radiographs revealed bone fragments in the stomach and intestines. The owner had been feeding raw chicken backs, necks, and wings. In another case, a golden retriever died from several small vertebral bodies, which had lodged in the lower end of the small intestines and perforated the intestinal wall. In another letter a woman lamented over the death of one of her shelties due to a ruptured esophagus after she fed him a raw meat and bone diet.

If you are feeding a raw diet and your pet displays symptoms such as severe vomiting, diarrhea, swollen abdomen, problems with swallowing, or any other unusual symptoms, seek veterinary attention immediately.

Things to Watch for with a Homemade Diet

In preparing a homemade diet for pets, you must be aware of a few dietary facts as they relate to companion animals. Although both dogs and cats will readily eat meat, cats are carnivores. Dogs can subsist on a vegetarian diet, but cats require a meat source of protein. Cats require much more protein than dogs, and kittens require more protein than a full-grown cat.

For dogs, vegetable protein does not contain all the amino acids that are required; therefore, a correct formulation of grains and other ingredients must be made if you plan on feeding your dog a vegetarian diet.

Indigestible proteins, such as those used in some commercial pet foods (hair, feathers, fecal matter), obviously cannot sustain an animal. Meat, fish, eggs (a complete source of protein), and dairy products provide many, if not all, the amino acids that your pet requires. Carbohydrates and fiber come primarily from grains and vegetables and provide energy and stamina and also provide calories to maintain weight. Grains should be cooked, and vegetables can be steamed or fed raw, and should be finely chopped or sliced, or run through a food processor. In this form, animals can more easily eat grains and vegetables.

Sunflower, corn, and safflower oil provide your pet with added energy, a lush coat, clear skin, and good muscle tone. Flaxseed and sesame oil, although more expensive, are excellent if your pet has an immune deficiency. Both these oils should be refrigerated to prevent them from becoming rancid. In the diet I prepare for my cats, I usually use safflower oil. In commercial pet food, legal sources of fiber can include hair, peanut hulls, beet pulp, and even ground-up paper. Pets eating a homemade diet obtain their fiber primarily from vegetables and fruit. One of my cats is rather old and prone to constipation, so I often add a teaspoon of natural bran to his food. My pets eat three meals a day: breakfast, lunch, and dinner. However, many pet owners feed their pets two meals per day, usually in the morning and in the evening.

Some nutritionists advise that pets should not eat protein, carbohydrates (grains), and vegetables at the same meal. Their reasoning is that when proteins and carbohydrates are ingested together, the protein is digested first, leaving the carbohydrates to digest later. According to Pat Lazarus, an animal nutritionist, this results in a build up of toxins due to the fermentation of the carbohydrates.

The ideal diet for your pets would include feeding meat or dairy products that can be combined with vegetables at one meal. Grains mixed with fruits and vegetables can be served at the next meal. In her book, *Keep Your Pet Healthy the Natural Way,* Lazarus recommends, "The only harmonious foods to be used with meats or even dairy proteins are vegetables (raw and grated or cut up)."[2]

However, my own personal experience over the last twelve years of cooking for my animal companions is that I have always fed protein, carbohydrates, and fruits or vegetables together. This has never caused any problem with any of my animals. My cats absolutely refuse to eat strictly grains mixed with fruit or vegetables at a meal. Ultimately, there are a lot of unknowns regarding a "complete and balanced" diet for dogs and cats, although there are many who claim they have the answers. Martin Goldstein, DVM, writes, "Our pets, like us, are all individuals, all with different requirements. So what works for one may not work for another."[3]

The diet for my dog is based on my own years of experience cooking for my animals as well as extensive information gathering. The following suggestions are not based on scientific evidence, but rather accumulated knowledge and sound advice from veterinarians and nutritionists who are knowledgeable about nutritional meals for cats and dogs.

A Natural Diet for the Dog

The diet for my dog includes:

⅓ protein, either cooked meat (beef, chicken, turkey, lamb), fish or eggs. Some dogs, including mine, are allergic to eggs. If you serve pork be sure that it is also well-cooked.

⅓ grains or carbohydrates, either brown rice (well-cooked), oatmeal, pasta, mashed potatoes, shredded wheat or other whole grain cereals, whole grain breads, plain or toasted. There is an array of grains to choose from, just be sure that they are well-cooked for proper digestion.

⅓ vegetables or fruits, including carrots, zucchini, peas, yellow and green beans, yams or sweet potatoes, mushrooms, apples, pears, watermelon—just about any fruit. Remember to chop or thinly slice the fruit and vegetables or run them through a food processor. Small amounts of cabbage, broccoli, and brussels sprouts can be used, but these vegetables tend to cause gas. My pets get their vegetables and fruit raw but I know of many people who lightly steam the vegetables. You can even use frozen vegetables, which retain a higher level of vitamins and minerals than do canned vegetables.

Vegetable oil. Depending on the size of the dog, one teaspoon to one tablespoon per day of vegetable oil. Again, flaxseed, sesame, sunflower, safflower, or olive oil (cold compressed).

For breakfast, my dog gets a bowl of oatmeal with a small amount of meat or fruit mixed in. Lunch and dinner are composed of meat, grains, and fruit or vegetables. With either lunch or dinner I add yogurt or cottage cheese for calcium. Plain, non-fat yogurt contains 450 mg. of calcium per cup. Yogurt is easily digested by pets and will replace the good bacteria in their systems if they are on antibiotics. Cottage cheese contains 155 mg. per cup. One cup of low-fat milk provides 300 mg. Calcium can also be obtained from other natural sources: 3 ounces of canned salmon with the bone contains 180 mg. of calcium and 3 1/2 ounces of sardines with bones, 400 mg. Two tablespoons of whole sesame seeds contain 175 mg. of calcium. Many vegetables contain calcium although in lower levels than the foods mentioned above.

How much calcium do our pets need per day? Martin Zucker quotes Nancy Scanlan, DVM, in his books, *Natural Remedies for Dogs* and *Natural Remedies for Cats:* "The recommended dosage for toy dogs is 100 mg. daily; small dogs, 200 mg.; medium dogs, 300 mg.; larger dogs, 500 mg. Large puppies can use 10 percent more."[4] She recommends the following for cats: "50 to 100 mg. daily. Increase the amount by 25 percent for kittens."[5] Dairy products provide calcium that is readily absorbed by both dogs and cats.

Riveriene Farm, a holistic nutrition website, describes various forms of calcium supplements in their Nutrition Index and notes that some of the calcium supplements can cause problems when added to a pet's diet. According to Riveriene Farm, bone-meal used in many dog food recipes, "contains absorbable calcium but may be contaminated with lead." You can purchase bonemeal that is certified free of heavy metal contamination, lead, mercury, and arsenic. If you are going to add a supplement, certified bonemeal is the best choice. The Nutrition Index describes calcium chloride as irritating to the intestinal tract, and calcium phosphate interferes with the absorption of other nutrients when included with other supplements. Neither calcium chloride nor calcium phosphate is a wise choice as a source of calcium for your pet. The conclusion reached in the Nutrition Index is that "the best sources of calcium are natural, organic food sources."[6]

In his book, *How to Have a Healthier Dog,* Wendell Belfield, DVM, advises, "It's too much, not too little that bothers me most in regard to calcium. Dog owners have this great urge to over-supplement calcium. A balanced vitamin and mineral supplement should contain all the extra calcium a growing dog or pregnant or lactating bitch needs."[7] Individual animals have individual needs. If you are going to supplement the diet of your dog or cat do so only under the guidance of your veterinarian.

My dog Sarge and my three cats enjoy a treat of bean sprouts, parsley, or alfalfa. These are sources of many minerals, vitamin C, and fiber. Your local health food store can usually provide a variety of seeds that you can grow in plastic or glass jars at home. It is a very easy process and you have an abundance of sprouts in no time. Mung beans are the most popular and lentils have an excellent mild flavor. Most sprouts will keep for seven to ten days in your refrigerator.

A Natural Diet for Cats

Feeding cats a natural diet can be a little more complex, especially if they have eaten commercial pet foods for most of their lives. Be assured it can be done, and they will enjoy their new diet just as much as the dog does.

Cats require more protein than dogs; therefore, their diet should be composed of two-thirds meat, and one-third grains and vegetables or fruit. Chicken and turkey seem to be the favorites with my cats, although every so often I open a can of salmon and they go wild. Fish of any kind is low in vitamin E, and vitamin E is required in high amounts by cats. Perhaps once a week you can give your cat some fish, which provides polyunsaturated fats that your cat cannot obtain from meat. Be careful in feeding tuna to your feline.

In her book *The Natural Cat,* Anitra Frazier describes the "tuna junkie" as an expression used by veterinarians to describe a cat hooked on tuna. According to Frazier, "The vegetable oil which it is packed in robs the cat's body of vitamin E which can result in a condition called steatitis."[8] Symptoms of steatitis include extreme nervousness and severe pain when touched. Lack of vitamin E causes nerve endings to become sensitive, and can also induce anemia and heart disease. However, excess levels of vitamin E can be toxic. A veterinarian with an understanding of nutrition should be consulted.

All meals for my cats are composed of protein, carbohydrates, and fiber plus a teaspoon of vegetable oil per day. This is all processed in the blender, but I hold back a few chunks of meat and add it to their food. This gives them something to chew on.

I usually add natural bran as a source of fiber. If your cat suffers from constipation, one half to one teaspoon of bran can be added to the diet. Constipation is a frequent problem in older cats. To help this, make sure water is always available for your animal companions.

Again, as with dogs, you can purchase a vitamin and mineral supplement for your cat if you feel they are not getting all the nutrients they require.

Despite what many veterinarians tell us about the problems encountered when we give our pets milk, I have given both my dog and cats milk (2 percent) for many years and none have developed diarrhea. I have taken into account their individual tastes and needs. Although my Siamese cats drink very little milk, my tabby drinks approximately one-half cup per day. As a pup, the veterinarian suggested that our German shepherd be given at least one cup of milk per day as a source of calcium for the puppy's developing bones. Sarge was given this amount for just over a year and now drinks about a half a cup per day.

Most veterinarians do not recommend that you give your pets milk although Richard Pitcairn in his book, *Dr. Pitcairn's Complete Guide to Natural Health for Dogs and Cats,* discusses giving your feline milk: "Some people recommend that raw milk and raw cheeses for the bulk of a cat's diet. Others say that cats, especially Siamese cats, do not properly digest lactose (milk sugar), and that drinking milk causes gas and diarrhea. Based on the feedback I solicit from clients, I have found that milk usually does not cause problems."[9] Dr. Pitcairn suggests using raw milk, yogurt, or goat's milk if your cat has problems digesting cow's milk. I would leave it to the discretion of pet owners or their veterinarian to decide if milk can be added to the animal's diet.

There is no doubt that a homemade diet, although time consuming, can add years to the life of your pets and save you a great deal of money in veterinary bills. Shawn Messonnier, author of numerous books on pet health, including *The Natural Health Bible for Dogs & Cats,* writes, "When it comes to feeding pets, dog and cat owners have two choices: prepare a fresh diet at home, or feed a processed food. When you can, feeding a homemade diet allows your pet to eat the freshest ingredients in their most tasty form."[10]

– NINE –

Vitamins, Minerals, and Supplements

Some experts say that it is not necessary to add supplements if you are providing your pet with a healthy, balanced diet of protein, grains, fiber, and fats. In order to be on the safe side, others advise adding a multi-vitamin and mineral specifically for cats or dogs. Martin Goldstein, DVM, states in his book, *The Nature of Animal Healing*, "I like to put young dogs and cats on chewable multivitamins—a regimen that, if combined with a healthy diet, ought to keep them disease-free within the first year of life."[1] He notes that only in cases of ill health does he resort to higher doses of one vitamin or another.

For example, vitamin C boosts the immune system by detoxifying certain carcinogens and by blocking the formation of various carcinogenic compounds created when certain foods are ingested. "Vitamin C may protect against cancer because it acts as a cellular antioxidant," explains Deborah Straw in her book, *Why Is Cancer Killing Our Pets?*[2] Dogs and cats do produce their own vitamin C but in times of illness and stress this vitamin can be depleted.

Shawn Messonnier, DVM, author of *The Natural Health Bible for Dogs & Cats*, provides in-depth information on vitamins, minerals, and supplements used in the treatment of various ailments in our pets. He warns, "Owners should not diagnose and treat their pets without veterinary supervision. Many medical disorders present similar symptoms. Also, megavitamin therapy can be toxic if not used properly."[3]

As my dogs age I do include extra vitamins in their diets. My dear animal companion, Charlie, was a Newfoundland who died in September 1997, just as my first book was published. The average lifespan of a Newfoundland is about eight years; however, Charlie lived to be fourteen. I gave him 1,500 mg. of vitamin C and 200 IU of vitamin E (d-alpha tocopherol) daily. There is no doubt in my mind that Charlie's natural diet and supplements added years to his life and kept him in good health. In 1999 I began to share my home with Sarge who was five years old at the time. He is a large, long-haired German shepherd who weighs about 130 pounds. Sarge suffers from an auto-immune disease, discoid lupus, so he is also taking additional vitamins and supplements. I believe the natural diet for the past four years plus the supplements have kept the discoid lupus under control.

In recent years, a growing number of concerned pet owners have decided to feed their pets a healthy diet. Most are willing to go that extra step and cook for their pets. However, many have been convinced that if they are going to feed a homemade diet they must add exotic substances, such as kelp, dandelion, fig powder, goldenseal, bee pollen, aloe, and more. This may not be necessary. Recently, I received a brochure from a California company that sells an extensive list of compounds and it states they *must* be added if feeding a natural diet to a dog or cat. To purchase all the suggested ingredients is very costly. In my opinion, if you are feeding your animal companion human-grade food, this should be sufficient for a healthy cat or dog.

However, if a pet is ill or suffering from allergies, the right vitamins and supplements are helpful. Be sure to consult with a holistic veterinarian educated in animal nutrition before mixing different supplements. Sometimes a mix of supplements can be harmful. For instance, excess bee pollen can cause more harm than good.

If you are feeding a commercial food or are concerned that your dogs are not getting all the nutrients they require from a homemade diet you can add a supplement to their diet. One that I found beneficial is K9-Rx, which provides high-quality protein, vitamins, minerals, and nutrients. Scott Connelly, MD, developed this supplement for dogs to be added to their regular food or as an added treat. In particular, K9-Rx also contains two nutrients not found in commercial foods, Methylsulfonyl-methane (MSM) and Lutein. MSM is a naturally occurring sulfur compound in animals (and humans) that supports joint and connective tissue health, which is extremely important as your pet ages. Lutein stimulates immune response in canines.

Vitamins and Minerals

Vitamins and minerals are as essential to the health of our companion animals as they are to our health. As with humans, it is far better to derive vitamins and minerals from the foods we eat rather than from supplements. However, this is not always possible, especially if your animal companion eats commercial pet foods.

Commercial pet food manufacturers add vitamins and minerals as a "premix," which I find highly questionable. How do heat and pressure in processing affect the availability of these compounds? I also question if the minerals are chelated or do they pass through the body unused if unchelated? (Chelation is the pharmaceutical process of bonding each mineral to an amino acid making it easier to digest and assimilate.) Vitamins are essential to normal growth; they aid in the conversion of food into energy, and form a necessary part of many hormones. Vitamins C, B, and A (beta-carotene) are water-soluble, and excesses are quickly eliminated from the body. Vitamins A (retinol), D, and E are fat-soluble vitamins and remain in the body for twenty-four hours. These vitamins can become concentrated in the liver. Because pet food companies often add vitamins and minerals as a premix, they are often not accurately measured and distributed evenly throughout the pet food. This means you can end up with doses of vitamins and minerals that are at higher or lower levels than what a cat or dog may need.

Nancy Scanlan, DVM, states, "While pets require supplementation for optimal health, it is important to remember that animal physiology is very different from humans." Scanlan adds,

"The safest and most effective means to meet the needs of your pet is to find a species-specific supplement or remedy from a trusted manufacturer who uses only human grade ingredients."[4]

If you are going to supplement your pet's diet with synthetic vitamins and minerals, be sure to consult a holistic veterinarian first. Both vitamins and minerals are required in minute amounts, so it is better to under-do than to over-do.

Vitamin A (Beta-carotene and Retinol) Vitamin A occurs in two forms: beta-carotene and retinol. Vitamin A in the form of beta-carotene is primarily in leafy green and yellow vegetables, carrots, dandelion greens (which contain five times the amount of vitamin A as carrots), sweet potatoes, broccoli, kale, and fruit. Excess amounts of beta-carotene can be toxic to humans and animals, however, since it is not fat soluble, it does not store in your body. Vitamin A in the form of retinol is the most active or usable form of vitamin A and is a fat soluble vitamin that stores up in your body. This form of vitamin A is derived from animal sources such as in fish liver oils, butter, cheese, egg yolks, liver, and whole milk.

Vitamin A, both beta-carotene and retinol, maintains healthy coat and skin, promotes bone growth, protects against infection, and aids in the treatment of eye disorders. Vitamin A deficiencies result in night blindness, susceptibility to infections, dryness and itching, and poor growth and development.

Vitamin B-1 (Thiamine) The B vitamins are water-soluble but, as with all vitamins and minerals, do not go overboard. Vitamin B-1 maintains normal function of the nervous system, and improves brain power in pets according to Wendell Belfield, DVM. In addition, some pet owners claim vitamin B-1 works as a flea repellent.

Vitamin B-1 is found in beef liver and kidneys, whole grains, bran oatmeal, salmon, wheat germ, peanuts, and kidney beans. Vitamin B-1 deficiencies may result in: unsteadiness, decreased learning ability, loss of appetite, fatigue, and vomiting.

Vitamin B-2 (Riboflavin) Vitamin B-2 maintains healthy mucous membranes, promotes growth and development, and contributes to healthy vision. Vitamin B-2 deficiencies may result in cataracts, sensitivity to light, dermatitis, and weakness in the hind legs. Vitamin B-2 is in cottage cheese, cheese, wheat germ, kidney, fish, and chicken.

Vitamin B-3 (Niacin) Vitamin B-3 maintains muscle tone, healthy skin, and coat. It converts food to energy and in some cases, prevents seizures. Vitamin B-3 deficiencies may result in black-tongue disease, muscle weakness, loss of appetite, and foul breath. Vitamin B-3 is in beef liver, white chicken meat, peanuts, salmon, tuna, turkey, whole grains, and milk.

Vitamin B-5 (Pantothenic Acid) Vitamin B-5 improves longevity, aids in wound healing, and protects against stress and infection. Vitamin B-5 deficiencies may result in nervousness, loss of appetite, and fatigue. Natural sources of vitamin B-5 include eggs, wheat germ, lentils, liver, brewer's yeast, peas, and whole grain products.

Vitamin B-6 (Pyridoxine) Vitamin B-6 promotes red-blood cell formulation, maintains a strong immune system, and contributes to a healthy nervous system. Vitamin B-6 deficiencies may result in weakness, nervousness, slow growth, weight loss, and inflammation of the skin. Vitamin B-6 is found in bananas, bran, brewer's yeast, carrots, salmon, tuna, wheat germ, lentils, and whole grain cereals

Vitamin B-12 (Cyanocobalamin) Vitamin B-12 is used to treat anemia, promotes normal growth and development, and stimulates weight gain in puppies. Deficiencies result in anemia, loss of appetite, pale mucous membranes, weakness, and fatigue. Vitamin B-12 is found in sardines, herring, milk products, eggs, organ meats, and beef.

Biotin Biotin is a lesser-known vitamin of the B family and is also known as vitamin H. This vitamin prevents skin problems, facilitates metabolism of amino acids and carbohydrates, and promotes the health of nerve cells. Biotin deficiencies may result in loss of appetite, anemia, and skin disorders. If the pet is on antibiotic or sulfa drugs, they may also develop a biotin deficiency. Biotin is found in brown rice, butter, tuna, eggs, chicken, cheese, liver, lentils, milk, and oats.

Vitamin C (Ascorbic Acid) Vitamin C is essential for the formation of collagen. It promotes tissue and wound healing, prevents infection, and can detoxify foreign substances entering the blood stream. Vitamin C can also reduce the pain of arthritis. Vitamin C deficiencies may result in swollen or painful joints, anemia, slow healing of wounds and tissue, foul breath, and loose teeth. The natural sources of vitamin C are oranges, peppers, tomatoes, broccoli, kiwi, rose hips, and strawberries. Basically, most fruits and vegetables supply vitamin C.

Vitamin D (Cholecalciferol) Vitamin D is fat-soluble vitamin. Sun exposure also provides vitamin D. This vitamin works with calcium and phosphorus to promote bone and tooth formation. Vitamin D deficiencies may result in malformation of bones and joints, and brittle bones. Vitamin D is in salmon, sardines, cod-liver oil, herring, and mackerel.

Vitamin E (Alpha-tocopherol) Vitamin E is a fat-soluble vitamin that acts as an anti-blood clotting agent. It also promotes muscle growth and repair, improves the immune system, promotes the healing of many skin problems, and improves the heart and circulatory system. Vitamin E deficiencies may result in muscle weakness, lethargy, and lack of energy.

Note: Vitamin E acts as an antioxidant and is often used as a preservative in natural pet foods. Vitamin E is found in wheat germ, whole wheat flour, margarine, corn oil, peanut oil, and eggs.

Vitamin K (Phytonadione) Vitamin K is fat-soluble vitamin that prevents abnormal bleeding. This vitamin is used in the treatment of dogs who have been poisoned with warfarin. Vitamin K deficiencies are rare. Vitamin K is in alfalfa, cheddar cheese, oats, spinach, and Brussels sprouts.

Minerals

Calcium and Phosphorus These two minerals are usually considered together due to their utilization in the body. Calcium provides strong bones and teeth, helps regulate blood clotting, and promotes the use of amino acids. Phosphorus also promotes strong bones and teeth. Calcium deficiencies may result in brittle bones, painful joints, poor appetite, soft teeth, and receding gums.

Note: Calcium and phosphorus ratios are about 1.2 to 1.4 parts of calcium to 1 part of phosphorus. Both require adequate amounts of vitamin D to be utilized by the animal's body.

Excess levels of calcium in the diet are a danger, since excess levels can cause accumulations on the bones. Kidney failure and constipation are also attributed to excess levels of calcium. Calcium and phosphorus are found in milk, cheese, canned salmon, bonemeal, legumes, meat, and eggs.

Chromium Chromium is a trace element that helps insulin in the regulation of blood sugar. Chromium deficiencies may result in cloudy eye corneas and sugar in the urine. Chromium can be found in dairy products, seafood, whole grain products, beef, chicken, and fresh fruits.

Cobalt Cobalt is also a trace mineral that promotes normal red blood cell formulation. This mineral is necessary for the production of vitamin B-12. Cobalt deficiencies may result in anemia, weight loss, fatigue, and weakness. Natural sources of cobalt are in liver, milk, spinach, kidney, eggs, and watercress.

Copper Copper promotes red blood cell formation. It is also a catalyst for the storage and release of iron for the formation of hemoglobin for red blood cells. Copper deficiencies may result in anemia, faulty collagen formation, and reproductive problems. Natural sources include mushrooms, oats, wheat germ, blackstrap molasses, salmon, and lentils.

Iodine Iodine promotes the normal function of the thyroid gland, aids in normal cell function, and keeps the skin and coat healthy. Iodine deficiencies may result in fatigue, sparse coat, and poor growth. Natural sources of iodine include table salt, kelp, canned salmon, cod, herring, haddock, and lobster.

Iron Iron forms part of the several proteins and enzymes in the body. It is especially important in guarding against anemia and poor growth in puppies. Iron deficiencies may result in fatigue, anemia, listlessness, and lowered resistance to disease and infections. Natural sources for iron include liver, egg yolks, wheat germ, whole grain products, cheese, blackstrap molasses, lentils, and enriched bread.

Magnesium Magnesium aids in bone growth, and the absorption of calcium and vitamins C, E, and B complex. It promotes healthy nerves and muscles. Magnesium deficiencies may result in skin problems, seizures, slow weight gain, and muscle weakness. Natural sources of magnesium are wheat germ, molasses, cod, carp, halibut, shrimp, green vegetables, and nuts.

Manganese Manganese aids in cell function, and promotes cartilage and bone growth. Manganese deficiencies may result in poor growth, and problems with the joints and discs. Natural sources of manganese include bran, peas, spinach, oatmeal, and seaweed.

Molybdenum Molybdenum, a rather rare mineral that is in minute concentrations in all plant and animal tissue. Molydbenum promotes normal growth, and healthy teeth and gums. Possible results of molybdenum deficiencies are unknown. Deficiencies of copper may involve molybdenum. Natural sources of molybdenum are cereal grains, liver, kidney, peas, and beans.

Potassium Sodium and potassium work together to maintain water balance in body tissue and cells. Potassium also promotes a regular heartbeat, and works in maintaining the transfer of nutrients to the cells. Potassium deficiencies may result in weakness, dehydration, slow growth, and irregular or rapid heartbeat. Natural sources of potassium are sardines, lentils, molasses, potatoes, parsnips, nuts, and whole grain cereals.

Selenium Selenium works with vitamin E as an antioxidant. It promotes healthy muscles, and is an essential element for healthy skin and coat. Selenium deficiencies may result in weight loss, poor skin and coat condition, and tooth decay. Natural sources of selenium are liver, milk, tuna, egg yolks, mushrooms, wheat germ, bran, whole grain cereals, chicken, and garlic.

Sodium Pets usually receive an adequate amount of salt through their diet and therefore adding salt is seldom necessary. Sodium regulates the fluid balance in the body and it is extremely important in maintaining blood pressure. Sodium deficiencies may result in muscle cramps, fatigue, hair loss, dry skin, and slow growth. The main source of sodium is table salt. Other sources include, ham, bacon, canned sardines, and snack foods.

Zinc Zinc is an antioxidant. Zinc promotes the healing of wounds and normal growth development. Zinc deficiencies may result in slow wound healing, decreased growth, poor appetite, and prostate problems in older dogs. Natural sources of zinc are whole-grain products, egg yolks, molasses, wheat germ, garlic, fish, turkey, and lamb.

Ten

Recipes for Cats and Dogs

Over the years, I have acquired a number of recipes for both dogs and cats, some of which you might enjoy preparing for your pet. Remember, pets are like people, they enjoy variety.

Most of these recipes are made in bulk or for one or two dogs or one or two cats. Use as little or as much as your dog or cat requires, depending on their size. Any grains or pasta must be cooked for proper digestion. Vegetables and fruit can be served raw although some pets prefer them steamed. Chop finely, slice thinly, or run the vegetables through a processor.

Beef, chicken, turkey, and lamb can be cut into chunks or you can purchase the ground meat. Cook the meat. Fish and eggs are also cooked or steamed. Once a week, you can serve liver, kidney or tripe—all cooked.

If possible, buy organic meats, since even human-grade meats sold in the typical grocery store are usually pumped up with hormones and antibiotics. In addition, if you buy meat from a natural food store, it is likely that the farm animals were raised on a sustainable farm, not a factory farm, and were treated humanely until slaughtered. (If you want to learn more about human meat production and the problems with factory farming in terms of animal welfare, health, and environment, read Dr. Michael Fox's book, *Eating with Conscience: The Bioethics of Food.*)

Be creative when cooking for your companion animals. Just be sure that your pet gets a recommended balance of protein, carbohydrates, and fats. I guarantee your animal companion will love you for the homecooked meal!

DOG MENU

Simple Recipe

3 cups cooked oatmeal or cream of wheat
2 cups cooked ground beef
2 tbsp. plain yogurt
1 small apple cut or sliced into small pieces

Mix together and serve. This meal can be served at breakfast, lunch, or dinner.

Chow Chow Chicken

2 chicken thighs or white meat
1 stalk celery, finely chopped
3 carrots, finely chopped
2 small potatoes, peeled and cubed
2 cups of rice, uncooked

Place chicken pieces in large pot. Cover with cold water. Add carrots, celery, and potatoes to water. Cover and simmer on low heat for about 2 hours until the chicken becomes tender. Add the rice. Cover and cook over low heat for about 30 minutes until the rice is tender and most of the liquid is absorbed. Remove from heat. Pull the chicken meat off the bone and discard bones. Return shredded pieces to pot and stir well. Let cool. Store in refrigerator or freeze.

SOURCE:
Deborah Smith
Kentucky

Sweet Potato Fritters

2 eggs
½ cup nonfat milk
2 tbsp. whole wheat flour
2 tbsp. wheat germ
2 cups raw sweet potatoes, finely grated
1 tbsp. olive oil

Beat eggs. Add milk. Mix in flour and wheat germ. Fold in grated sweet potatoes. Fry over medium heat until cooked all the way through.

SOURCE:
Katie Merwick
People Food for Dogs

Macaroni, Liver, and Veggie Dinner

2 cups of elbow macaroni, cooked
2 pieces of beef liver cooked in butter or oil
1 can of mixed vegetables, drained
1 cup of cottage cheese

Chop liver slices in pieces. Add macaroni and vegetables. Fold in cottage cheese. Serve.

Weimaraner Walleye Recipe

3 pounds walleye pike fillets
2 oz. chicken livers, diced finely
2 cups fish stock
3 cups cooked brown rice
¼ cup cooked wild rice
¼ cup kale, frozen
½ cup green beans, frozen
½ cup collard greens, frozen
½ cup corn, frozen
¼ cup potatoes, frozen
1 tbsp. cod liver oil

Preheat oven to 350°F. In a baking dish add walleye fillets and diced chicken livers. Pour in fish stock and cod liver oil. Add frozen veggies, and cover and bake for 20 to 30 minutes or until done. In a large bowl add cooked rice and the juices from the baking dish along with the cooked veggies. Mix well. Chunk the walleye into a size for your dog and mix well. Allow to cool, then serve. Freeze leftovers or keep refrigerated.

SOURCE:
Doggie Connection
www.doggieconnection.com/recipe/

Beef Stew

1 16 oz. can of low-sodium beef broth
2 tsp. onion powder
2 tsp. garlic, minced
2 carrots, chopped
2 stalks celery, chopped
1 cup peas
1 cup steak cubes, cooked
2 tbsp. cold water
½ to 1 tsp. cornstarch

Bring broth, onion powder, and garlic powder to a boil. Add vegetables and beef. Simmer 20 minutes. Combine cold water and cornstarch. Stir into stew.

SOURCE:
Katie Merwick
People Food for Dogs

Pensioner's Birthday Party Casserole

1 cup cooked turkey or chicken
2 tbsp. bacon fat or vegetable oil
8 lasagne noodles
1 egg
1 tbsp. wheat germ oil
1 tsp. bone meal
¼ tsp. garlic powder

Cook noodles as directed on package. Drain. Line bottom of 8x8-inch pan. In medium-sized bowl, mix chopped turkey or chicken with bacon fat, egg, wheat germ oil, and bone meal. Spoon over noodles and spread. Cover with layer of noodles and sprinkle with garlic powder. Bake 30 minutes in 350°F oven. Let stand for 15 minutes before cutting.

SOURCE:
Edmund R. Dorosz, BSA, DVM
Let's Cook for Our Dogs

Weight Reduction Diet for Adult Dogs

½ lb. chicken (raw weight), cooked
2 cups rice, long-grain, cooked
¼ tsp. salt substitute (potassium chloride)
A dash of table salt
4 bonemeal tablets
1 multiple vitamin-mineral tablet

Mix all ingredients.

SOURCE:
Donald R. Strombeck, DVM
Home Prepared Dog and Cat Diets

Chinese Style Dinner

2 cups of cooked brown rice
1 cup cooked ground chicken
1 cup grated carrots, zucchini, or celery

Mix together, add 1 tbsp. vegetable oil and top with alfalfa sprouts.

Canine Meat and Grain Bulk Menu

12 cups cooked brown rice
2 cups fatty meat (regular ground hamburger, fatty beef heart, beef chuck roast)
2 cups lean meat (chicken hearts, ground turkey, beef and chicken liver, whole chicken or turkey, lean beef heart)
1 ½ cups grated or chopped vegetables

Mix all ingredients together; or, steam meat and vegetables and then add rice. Serve the daily ration slightly warm.

SOURCE:
Richard Pitcairn, DVM, PhD
Natural Health for Dogs and Cats

Spaghetti with Meat Sauce

8 oz. whole wheat spaghetti cooked and drained
1 lb. hamburger fried
4 medium mushrooms cut in pieces
1 medium tomato, chopped
½ cup tomato juice

Mix hamburger with mushrooms, celery, and chopped tomato Stir in tomato juice. Pour over spaghetti and serve warm.

Lamb and Rice Allergy Diet

1 lb. ground lamb
2 cups cooked brown rice
½ cup chopped parsley
1 cup grated zucchini
½ cup of plain yogurt

Steam or fry lamb in two tablespoons of oil. Add rice, parsley, zucchini. Just before serving mix in ½ cup of yogurt.

Milk Replacement Recipe for Puppy

1 cup (3 ½% fat) cow or goat milk
1 egg yolk
2 drops infant vitamins (human)
1 tsp. corn oil
2 drops cod liver oil

Mix and refrigerate. Warm to body temperature before feeding. Feed as much as the puppy will eat or when their tummies are full and they are content.

SOURCE:
Edmund R. Dorosz, BSA, DVM
Let's Cook for Our Dog

Veggie Pot Pie

Crust:
2 ¼ cups flour
⅓ cup cold water
¼ cup vegetable oil
¼ tsp. salt

Pie ingredients:
2 cans cream of potato condensed soup
1 cup of milk
¼ tsp. thyme leaves crushed
¼ tsp. pepper
4 cups cooked cut vegetables

Preheat oven to 400°F. Combine crust ingredients. Separate into two balls. Roll into two 9x13-inch crusts. Lay one crust on bottom of greased 9x13-inch baking dish.

Mix other ingredients in bowl. Spread vegetable mixture evenly on top of crust. Lay second crust on top of vegetable mixture. Bake 30 minutes or until crust is golden. Let stand 10 minutes before serving.

SOURCE:
Sweetie's Yorkie Web World
www.geocities.com/Hearland/Pointe/9350/recipes.html

Convalescing Diet

If your dog has undergone surgery or is recovering from an illness this is easy on the stomach.

2 cups of cooked cream of wheat
1 soft boiled egg
1 ½ cups cottage cheese
¾ cup grated parsnips
1 tbsp. melted butter

Mix together and serve warm.

CAT MENU

Cats require more protein than a dog. In addition, cats also choose one or two diets they like and tend to ignore other foods you may offer them.

Chicken, Rice, and Vegetables

2 cups of ground or chopped chicken, cooked
1 cup of cooked brown rice
¼ cup grated carrots

Cut chicken into small pieces. Run carrots through food processor. Mix chicken and carrots with rice and if there is any fat from the chicken, pour about two teaspoons over the mix. Serve at room temperature.

Sole Dinner

½ lb. fillet of sole
2 tbsp. onion, chopped
  (optional)
2 tbsp parsley, chopped
Enough water to cover
  bottom of dish
1 tbsp. butter
1 tbsp. flour

½ cup milk
¼ tbsp. cheddar cheese,
  grated
2 tbsp. liver
¼ tsp. iodized salt
⅔ cup cooked noodles, cut
into kitty-bite size pieces (or
cooked rice)

Put sole in a small, greased baking dish. Sprinkle with parsley. Add enough water to cover the bottom of dish. Cook in a pre-heated 450° F. oven for 10 minutes. Remove from oven and cool. Cut into kitty-size pieces. Melt butter in small saucepan. Stir in flour and heat until bubbling. Gradually stir in milk and cook, stirring constantly until mixture thickens. Add cheese, liver, and salt. Stir until cheese has melted. Do not boil. Add chopped fish and noodles to cheese sauce and stir. Cool and serve.

SOURCE:
Tony Lawson
The Cat-Lovers' Cookbook

Bland Diet for Finicky Felines

1 cup boiled chicken
¼ cup broccoli, steamed
¼ cup shredded carrots, steamed
Chicken broth, approximately half a cup

Mix ingredients with enough chicken broth to hold it together. Recipes can also be used with fish instead of chicken.

Spot's Stew

This recipe is based on Spot's Stew canned food, which Halo, Purely for Pets, produces. This company is mentioned in Chapter Eight.

1 whole chicken
16 oz. brown rice
7 or 8 carrots
6 or 7 stalks of celery
2 or 3 yellow squash
2 or 3 zucchini
1 small crown of broccoli
A handful of green beans
5 or 6 garlic cloves

Wash chicken and place in a large stew pot. Cover with water. Cut all veggies into pieces, and add to the stew pot along with the rice. Cover and cook for 1 ½ to 2 hours, depending on the size of the chicken. Once the chicken is well-cooked, debone. Pour veggies, rice, broth, and chicken into the blender and puree into kitty-size pieces. This can be put in sealable plastic bags and frozen. Remove and thaw as needed.

Kitty Breakfast

1 tbsp. nonfat dry milk
3 medium eggs
3 tbsp. cottage cheese
2 tbsp. grated veggies or sprouts

Mix the milk powder with a little water and beat with the eggs. Cook in a hot pan. When mixture is cooked, turn it over, and put the cottage cheese and veggies or sprouts on top. When this is firm, fold it over like an omelet. Cut into bite-size pieces for your kitties.

Salmon and Rice Diet

5 oz. salmon, canned with bones
½ large egg, hard boiled
⅓ cup rice, long-grain, cooked
1 calcium carbonate tablet (400 mg. calcium)
1 multiple vitamin-mineral tablet

Mix together and serve.

SOURCE:
Donald R. Strombeck, DVM, PhD
Home Prepared Dog and Cat Diets

Liver Feast

2 cups chopped beef or chicken liver
2 tbsp. vegetable oil
1 cup cooked oatmeal
¼ cup frozen peas, steamed

Cook liver in vegetable oil and chop finely. Add cooked oatmeal and peas. Cool and serve at room temperature.

Leftovers

1 ½ cup leftover meat, beef, chicken, turkey, lamb,
    finely chopped.
½ cup leftover veggies, carrots, zucchini, sweet potato,
    squash, or sprouts
¾ cup mashed potatoes, rice, or oatmeal
1 tbsp. vegetable oil

Run veggies through processor. Chop meat finely. Add
meat to veggies and potatoes, rice, or oatmeal. Stir in vegetable
oil and serve.

Tuna Lunch

1 6 ½ oz. can of tuna packed in oil
½ cup cooked brown rice
¼ cup grated carrots
2 tbsp. of wheat germ (vitamin E)

Blend and serve at room temperature. Do not serve more
than once a week since tuna can deplete vitamin E.

Liver and Kidney Dinner

1 cup cooked or ground liver or kidney
¾ cup cooked oatmeal
3 tbsp. grated carrots or zucchini
⅓ cup plain yogurt
3 tsp. of butter

Mix ground meat, oatmeal, and vegetables together. Melt
butter and pour over mixture. Stir in yogurt and serve at room
temperature.

Salmon Feast

1 15 oz. can of salmon
1 cup cooked brown rice
¼ cup chopped parsley or celery
3 tbsp. of plain yogurt

　　Drain salmon. Mix in brown rice, vegetables, and yogurt. Serve at room temperature.

Get Well Feast

1 cup of leftover beef (cooked)
¼ cup alfalfa or parsley
½ cup cooked cream of wheat
¼ cup creamed cottage cheese

　　Blend and process ingredients into a thin consistency. Serve warm.

Allergy Diet

2 cups ground lamb
½ cup grated carrots or zucchini
1 cup cooked brown rice
¼ cup cottage cheese
¼ tsp. garlic powder

　　Combine all ingredients and either mix in blender or serve as is at room temperature.

Newborn Kitten Diet

Should you have to feed newborn kittens, mix undiluted canned evaporated milk with a few tablespoons of plain yogurt. This mixture can be refrigerated and warmed as needed at feeding time. Goat's milk is an excellent substitute.

Kitten Supplement

A recipe that is used by breeders for orphaned kittens.

12 oz. of water
1 envelope of Knox Gelatin
1 12 oz. can of whole evaporated milk (not skim)
2 tbsp. mayonnaise
2 tbsp. plain yogurt (not nonfat)

Boil the water, add the gelatin, stir well. Add following ingredients in order, mixing well after each addition.

½ of the canned milk (6 oz.)
2 tbsp. of mayonnaise and 2 tbsp. of yogurt
Add the rest of the milk

You could also include a kitty vitamin and/or pureed baby food meat, lamb, chicken, or beef.

CRUNCHIES FOR DOGS AND CATS

Perhaps your pet likes crunchy food. These are a couple of recipes that I make and feed both the dog and cats.

1 ½ cups whole wheat flour
1 ½ cups rye flour
1 ½ cups brown rice flour
1 cup wheat germ
1 tsp. dried kelp or alfalfa
4 tbsp. vegetable oil
1 tsp. garlic powder
1 ¼ cups beef or chicken broth or stock

Mix dry ingredients. Slowly add broth and vegetable oil. Roll out into a thin sheet. Place on cookie sheet and bake at 350°F. until golden brown. Cool and break into bite-size pieces. Toss lightly in catnip or brewer's yeast. Store in air-tight container in refrigerator.

Chicken Crunchies

1 ½ lbs. chicken wings, necks, backs, and liver, cooked and ground
1 15 oz. can of salmon, mackerel, or tuna in oil
1 ½ cups rye flour
2 cups whole wheat flour
2 ½ cups brown rice flour
1 ½ cups wheat germ
5 tbsp. vegetable oil
2 tsp. garlic powder
4 tbsp. powdered kelp
1 ½ cups powdered milk
¾ cups brewer's yeast
4 cups of beef or chicken stock

Mix dry ingredients. Mix in ground chicken and fish. Mix beef or chicken stock with vegetable oil. Blend into dry mix. Roll to ¼" thickness and place on cookie sheet. Bake at 350°F. until golden brown. Break into pieces. Store in air-tight container in refrigerator.

– ELEVEN –

Other Toxic Products

Each day animal companions, like children, encounter dangers and it is up to us to do our best to protect them. Some of those daily dangers include plants—indoor and outdoor—that can be harmful to dogs and cats. Lawn sprays used to keep the grass weed-free can also be highly toxic for animal companions, as well as humans. Anti-freeze from cars can kill a cat after just a few licks. Cats can have serious problems if they ingest that convenient and easy-to-handle clumping litter, and the dogs can suffer, too, if they get into the cat box. Even some of the dog treats that we think are harmless can cause death in extreme cases. And some of the foods we eat, and want to share with our pets, can contain substances that cause severe allergies. The following are the more important items to watch out for.

Outdoor and Indoor Plants

I always thought of myself as conscientious when bringing plants into my home. I avoided plants that might harm cats and dogs if they happened to chew on them. Just over a year ago, I bought a large succulent plant at a garage sale. The seller advised keeping the plant outdoors in the summer, then bring it inside in the fall, and it would flower just after Christmas. She did not know the name of the plant, and although I was familiar with the leaves, I did not know what kind of plant it was nor did anyone else I asked. It hung in my garden all summer and in the late fall I brought it in and stood it in a planter in my living room. Shortly after Christmas it began to bloom clusters of small red flowers.

My old Siamese, Ben, had been diagnosed with hyperthyroidism shortly before Christmas and was on drugs to control this disease plus another medication to lower his heart rate. Shortly after being on the drugs Ben became inactive, ate very little, and vomited at least twice a day. His weight dropped and after numerous visits to the vet we finally decided to take him off the drugs. Even this did not seem to work.

One morning when I returned home from shopping my son told me that Ben had thrown up the catnip I had fed him. However, I had not given Ben or the other cats any catnip. I checked all my plants and they all seemed to be untouched. That evening as I watched television Ben got up on a chair beside the plant and bit into some of the leaves, but did not really eat them. Within an hour he began to vomit again.

I removed the plant from the room and put it in the basement where Ben could not get at it until I found out what kind of a plant I had brought home. The next morning, after going through numerous books I found that this was a kalanchoe plant. I checked the National Animal Poison Control Center for its list of plants that might be toxic but did not find kalanchoe. Checking the website for the American Society for the Prevention of Cruelty to Animals (AVMA), "Poison Control Center's Household Plant Reference," I found a list that labeled the kalanchoe plant as a "cardiotoxic plant." The AVMA site described various plants that could be fatal, which included hydrangea, lily-of-the-valley, castor bean, foxglove, and kalanchoe. That day my sister, who has no pets, became the owner of this plant. Over the next few days Ben improved. He began eating, the vomiting ceased, he was more active, and was back on his drug for hyperthyroidism. Because I did not know and I assumed that the cats would not bother with this plant, I could have killed Ben.

As a result of that close call with Ben, I have listed some of the plants identified by the National Animal Poison Control Center that can be toxic to cats and dogs. In many cases it is not only the leaves of the plants that can be toxic but also the seeds, stems, or fruit they produce. Plants that may not cause a problem in dogs can cause serious illness or even death in cats. This is not a complete list, but it is worth having if you have a pet and also love plants. For an extensive list of toxic plants visit one of these websites:

www.cherishedmoments.com/poisonous-plants-dogs.htm
www.cherishedmoments.com/poisonous-plants-cats.htm

The following house plants can cause severe symptoms, including vomiting, diarrhea, seizures, heart failure, or death in dogs and cats.[1]

- English Holly
- Boston Ivy, English Ivy, and Needlepoint Ivy
- Poinsettia
- Mistletoe
- Kalanchoe
- Dieffebbachia (Dumbcane)
- Philodendron
- Schefflera
- Peace Lily
- Asparagus Fern (cats)
- Amaryllis
- Weeping Fig

The following outdoor plants are toxic to both dogs and cats.

- Chrysanthemum
- Tomato leaves and stems
- Rhubarb leaves
- Morning Glory
- Nightshade
- Boxwood
- Hemlock
- Larkspur
- Lily of the Valley
- Foxglove
- Geranium
- Daffodil
- Primrose
- Easter Lily (especially toxic for cats)

Safe Plants

Some safe plants to have in your home include, African violet, spider plant, Boston fern, donkey tail, lipstick plant, ponytail palm, sword fern, prayer plant, grape ivy, button fern, carrot fern, zinnia, snapdragon, rabbit's foot fern, orchid, gerbena daisy, coleus, piggyback plant, bottlebrush, and baby tears, to name a few.

Lawn Sprays

A herbicide, 2,4-Dichlorophenoxyacetic Acid (2,4-D), which is used by homeowners and lawn care companies, has been linked to canine malignant lymphoma. This study, which was undertaken by the National Cancer Institute, determined, "The risk of canine lymphoma rose to a twofold excess with four or more yearly applications of 2,4-D. This herbicide has also been implicated as the source of nonHodgkin's disease in humans."[2]

The herbicide, 2,4-D is found in one-third of all pesticides and is a component of Agent Orange. Homeowners and farmers use this herbicide for weed control because it is cheaper and more effective than other weed killers. Doctors urge people using this herbicide to wear masks, boots, and gloves for protection.

At the same time humans are taking precautions around this herbicide, cats and dogs can walk across the lawn sprayed with this chemical, unprotected. At the present time 2,4,-D "is under special review by the Environmental Protection Agency in the United States because of concerns about chronic health and environmental effects."[3] In addition to being a toxic threat to animals and humans, chemical fertilizers and pesticides on lawns weaken the grass and destroy the natural balance of microbes and beneficial insect predators, thus, in the end promoting weed and insect proliferation.

As an alternative, try an organic fertilizer, which slowly feeds your lawn and does not kill earthworms. Mow your lawn at the mower's highest setting and let the grass cuttings stay in the lawn as a natural mulch. You could even spend some time outside and pull up weeds or use one of the new contraptions that just pops them out of the ground.

Think twice before spraying toxic chemicals on your lawn. Cats walking on a sprayed lawn lick their paws, ingesting this toxic substance. Dogs walk and roll in grass sprayed with these chemicals and if they have even a small cut, these toxins can enter their system. Our health, the health of our animal companions, and the health of the environment are at risk when we apply these toxic chemicals. Is it worth having the perfect weed-free lawn at the expense of our health and the health of our animal companions?

Bones and Dried Pet Chews

At one time or another most of us have given our dogs a bone, pig ears, or cow hooves to chew on, but have any of us considered how dangerous this might be? Bones of any kind, raw or cooked, chicken, turkey, beef, and pork bones are easily chewed into sharp splinters, which can lodge in the gastrointestinal tract and may cause esophageal or intestinal lacerations. Bones have also been shown to cause perforations and even complete obstructions.

According to the veterinary dentists I interviewed for my second book, *Protect Your Pet,* such bones can also cause severe damage to teeth. Fraser Hale from the Veterinary College at Guelph, Canada, feels it is a mistake to think that just because your dog has white teeth from chewing on a bone that the teeth are healthy. In an article for *Dogs in Canada,* Dr. Hale writes, "It is true that dogs that routinely chew on bones will tend to have clean tooth crowns; however, they're also very prone to having fractured teeth. These fractures typically expose the pulp tissue inside the tooth and allow infection to travel through the root-canal system and into the jawbone."[4]

Dr. Hale also notes that this is not only a painful condition but it also constitutes an open pathway for infection to enter the body. Only dental X-rays can detect this condition since there is usually no bleeding gum tissue or foul odor that would alert the owner. Brushing your dog or cat's teeth is the only safe way to prevent plaque build up and dental disease. If brushing becomes routine when they are puppies or kittens, they soon learn that this task can be enjoyable.

One product that has been around for many years, "Nylabone Plaque Attacker," claims to remove plaque from teeth. However, in the last few years Nylabone products have also come under scrutiny because of the deaths of dogs who have eaten Nylabone. The Nylabone Plaque Attacker and Gumma-Bone are made of flexible material which, when swallowed, could become lodged somewhere in the intestinal tract. In November 2001, the company pulled the Plaque Attacker from the shelves. Many people still have these and I advise that they dispose of them. The manufacturer of Nylabone has announced that it will be introducing a new product to replace the one discontinued.

A lucrative line of pet treats made from parts of animals, such as pig ears, cow hooves, and turkey necks, grace the shelves of pet stores. These treats are processed with chemicals, treated with preservatives, and infused with artificial flavorings. If these treats are swallowed whole they can cause choking or large pieces may become lodged in the throat and esophagus. Many pet owners have reported pets vomiting or developing severe diarrhea after ingesting these pet treats. In late 1999 the Food and Drug Administration issued a nationwide public health warning to alert consumers that these treats could pose a risk of bacterial infection such as Salmonella. The warning was aimed at the consumer who handles the product although there is clear evidence that pets are also susceptible to such bacterial infection.

If you are going to give your pet treats, look for healthy alternatives. There are many dog treats out there that are made with healthy ingredients. Dog cookies made with whole grains and vegetables and without additives and preservatives are available at most pet shops. I have included some recipes for these tasty delights in Chapter Ten. You can purchase roles of cut and bake cookies for dogs that contain only human-grade ingredients. You could even give them fresh carrots, fresh green beans, or chunks of apple to munch on, depending on your dog's preferences.

Monosodium Glutamate (MSG)

Many humans have allergies to the food enhancer, MSG, but did we ever consider our pets could also have a reaction to MSG? Although rare, there have been cases of dogs experiencing severe reactions after ingesting foods that contain this substance. Reactions can occur immediately or up to forty-eight hours after the pet ingests the food enhancer. MSG reactions are often misdiagnosed as epileptic seizures. A pet could end up on medication for the rest of his or her life because the veterinarian diagnosed the problem based on the symptoms.

If your pet is experiencing seizures there are a couple of things you might do. First, if you are feeding commercial foods, check the label to see if it contains textured protein, yeast extract, hydrolyzed protein, glutamic acid, gelatin, or sodium or calcium caseinate. These substances always contain MSG. Other ingredients that often contain MSG include whey protein, soy protein, soy sauce, carrageenan or vegetable gum, anything fermented, chicken, beef or pork smoke flavorings.

Human food can also be a source of MSG. According to an article by Jeff Gordy on MSG, a lot of restaurants may use MSG to prepare their food, including McDonalds, Burger King, Kentucky Fried Chicken, and many others.[5]

Clumping Kitty Litter

Clumping kitty litters are supposed to reduce odor and help in absorption but how safe are these products for our cats? One of the ingredients in these products is sodium bentonite, which makes the litter clump and makes it easier for disposal. In *The Complete Guide to Vegetarian Convenience Foods,* author Gail Davis explains, "Bentonite is a clay formed by the decomposition of volcanic ash that has the ability to absorb large quantities of water and to expand to several times its normal volume."[6]

Clumping kitty litter also contains silica dust, a known cancer-causing agent. Davis notes, "When poured into your cat's litter box, and kicked up by your cat, silica dust rises into the air posing the risk of bronchial and respiratory infections."[7]

According to the "Pet Consumer Report," an online publication, when your cat digs in the litter, "the dust from the litter gets into the cat's lungs and can wreak havoc on its immune system, putting his or her health in jeopardy."[8] Inhaling this silica dust is not good for humans either. Prolonged exposure to silica dust causes silicosis in humans and animals, a sometimes-fatal lung disease.

Some of these kitty litter products post a clear warning on their products, "Do Not Let Cat Ingest Litter." Anyone who owns a cat knows what fastidious creatures they are and to what great lengths they go grooming themselves. It is highly likely that cats ingest kitty litter when they are cleaning themselves. Once the kitty litter is inside the cat or kitten it expands and can cause dehydration by absorbing the body's moisture. Clumping kitty litter can also form a hard mass in the intestines over a period of time that could be fatal. This dangerous situation can extend to dogs as well if you have a dog who likes to get into the litter box for occasional "snacks."

So what are the alternatives? There are now a number of biodegradable litters on the market made from natural blends of wheat grass fibers, recycled wood products that are pure sawdust, plant material, corn granules, whole wheat products, and paper-milling by-products. Some excellent alternative products available on the market are listed in *The Complete Guide to Vegetarian Convenience Foods*. The author researched products that are safe for animals as well as environmentally friendly. Some of these products can be found in stores and some purchased through mail order.

If you are concerned about the odor from some of the biodegradable litters, you can sprinkle about a teaspoon of baking soda in with the litter. Baking soda works better than the deodorizers in clumping litters, plus it is safer. These deodorizers can be toxic, and can cover up the odors but the baking soda will absorb them and it is nontoxic. Read labels and make sure that the product contains no deodorizers, colors, or drying agents that could be potentially harmful to your cat.

A good hint for changing the brand of litter with finicky cats is to do this slowly. Perhaps begin by mixing one-fourth of the new biodegradable litter with the familiar kitty litter. Over time, your cat will adjust to the switch.

Anti-Freeze

Anti-freeze, a very toxic substance to our pets, is made with ethylene glycol. It has a sweet taste that pets find appealing. Within an hour of ingesting anti-freeze, animals can display symptoms including anxiety, vomiting, depression, and weakness. These are caused by the corrosive chemical destroying the animal's kidneys and entering the blood stream. In six to eighteen hours this can progress to a comatose state and death within another six to eighteen hours. Ethylene glycol is so toxic that even a small amount, which cats may lick off their paws, is fatal. The amount to kill a dog is slightly more. If you suspect that your pet has ingested anti-freeze seek veterinary attention immediately. Your pet could be saved if he is treated within *fifteen minutes* of ingesting this substance. After that, it may be too late.

If you are using anti-freeze make sure you clean up any spills completely and never pour it into a stream or onto the ground. Check driveways and garages to make sure a radiator has not leaked anti-freeze.

There now are pet-safe anti-freeze products that contain propylene glycol instead of the toxic ethylene glycol. There are also products that incorporate a bitter tasting substance. For a few dollars more I strongly recommend that you use these products. Also, if a car mechanic replaces the anti-freeze, ask that he or she use a pet-safe product. This could save your pet's life.

– TWELVE –

Consumer Action

We have the right and the obligation as consumers to know what we are buying from pet food companies that claim their product provides a complete and balanced nutritional diet. I know that pet lovers would never intentionally buy any product that would harm the health of their animal companions. However, the days of trusting the advertisements are gone. Consumers need to ask questions and know as specifically as possible *what* is in the food they are feeding their pets. The health and welfare of our animal companions are in our hands, which means we cannot blindly trust what slick advertising would have us believe nor should we depend on obscure labeling.

Unquestionably, the commercial pet food industry provides consumers with vague terms that mask what is actually in the food and what can legally be included as ingredients. Many consumers have contacted me to ask about specific pet foods, and I always encourage them to contact the pet food company directly. Often, they are stonewalled or receive more vague information. Nonetheless, consumers need to continue to question pet food manufacturers to find out what really is in the pet food.

If you are going to feed a commercial pet food and want to be sure that it is a quality product I have compiled a list of questions that you might ask the pet food companies. Don't be fooled by the names of pet foods, some of which may sound scientific and legitimate. And don't be satisfied just because the label reads "USDA Inspected"—this means very little. This phrase can mean that it is inspected and passed as fit for human consumption—or inspected and condemned.

If the pet food company refuses to reply to your query or if it provides a standard reply, such as "our meat is government inspected," or "we use quality grains and fats," then go further with your questions. Ask for more specific information, such as, "Do you use human-grade ingredients?" If the company cannot provide satisfactory information, don't feed it to your pet.

Depending on your level of concern, you may ask some or all of the following questions.

Questions About Protein

1. What parts of the animal are used in your food product?
2. Is the meat coming from federally inspected facilities?
3. Is the meat inspected and approved as fit for human consumption?
4. Is the meat denatured in any way?
5. What preservatives are used on the meat?
6. Is the raw product tested for Salmonella, Listeria, Campylobacter, E. coli?
7. Is the meat free from antibiotics and hormones? (Keep in mind that most grocery store meat for humans contains antibiotics and hormones. You must buy organic to avoid these.)
8. Is the testing of the meat undertaken at the slaughterhouse and also your facility?
9. If the product contains "meat meal" what is the composition of this meat meal?

Questions About Meat Meal and Lamb

1. Is the lamb meal used coming from scrapie-free countries? (The only two countries that are scrapie-free are Australia and New Zealand.)
2. Is the meal coming from federally inspected facilities?
3. Is the meat in the meal classified as fit for human consumption?

4. What part(s) of the animal are used in the meal?

5. Is the meat denatured at the point of origin?

6. Is the raw material tested for Salmonella, Listeria, Campylobacter, E. coli?

Questions About Grains

1. Are whole grains used?

2. If not, what part(s) of the grains are used?

3. Are the grains tested for levels of mycotoxins?

4. Are the grains tested by the mill and also at your facility?

Questions About Fats

1. What are the sources of fats?

2. What agent is used as a preservative?

Questions About Fiber

1. What are the sources of fiber used in your foods?

2. Are the sources listed on the label the only sources of fiber in the product?

General Questions

1. Does every batch of pet food contain the same ingredients?

2. Is the meat meal tested for levels of sodium pentobarbital?

3. Do you adhere to AAFCO or CVMA guidelines?

Remember, many pet food companies also produce an extensive line of private label foods and prescription diets. Check the label of the food you are using for the name of the company. Most companies list an 800 number on the label. Call the number, ask for the name of the president/CEO, and address questions to him/her.

Do not address your questions or concerns to the company in general. You will get the standard pat answers that tell you nothing. Write to the president, chairperson, or CEO of the company. If their responses are not acceptable, restate your concerns and expectations, and try again. Most names and addresses can be obtained from the company's website. Below are a list of names and addresses of some of the larger companies in the United States.

Most likely you will receive a lengthy, evasive reply that feels like a pat on the head. Don't be deterred. Write again, making it clear that you want the issues addressed. Keep writing until you are satisfied. If you are lucky, you may receive a second reply, most likely still evasive, and you will hear no more. "Ignore them and they'll go away," seems to be the typical mode of this industry.

Next step, go to the agencies responsible for the industry. These agencies have no government affiliation. They are composed of members of the pet food industry and can provide the addresses for pet food companies in the United States, Canada, and the United Kingdom.

Pet Food Companies
IN THE UNITED STATES

Colgate Palmolive – Hill's Science Diet
Robert Wheeler, CEO
1035 Northeast 43rd Street
Topeka, KS 66617

Heinz Pet Products – Nature's Recipe Dog and Cat Food
William Johnson, CEO
339 Sixth Avenue
Pittsburgh, PA 15201

Nestlé Purina-Ralston Purina Company
W. Patrick McGinnis, President and CEO
Checkerboard Square
St. Louis, MO 63164

Nutro Products, Inc.
Ladd Hardy, Vice President for Marketing
445 Wilson Way
City of Industry, CA 91744

Proctor & Gamble Iams – Iams Pet Food
Dr. Dan Carey, Veterinary Nutritionist
7250 Poe Avenue
Dayton, OH 45414

Pet Food Organizations
IN THE UNITED STATES
Pet Food Institute
Duane Ekedahl, Executive Director
Nancy Cook, Director, Technical and Regulatory Affairs
2025 M Street N.W., Suite 800
Washington, D.C. 20036

IN CANADA
Pet Food Association of Canada
345 Banbury Road
Toronto, Ontario M2L 2V2

IN THE UNITED KINGDOM
The Pet Food Manufacturers' Association
20 Bedford Street,
London, England WC2E 9HP

Government Organizations
The only U.S. government agency that has any input into the ingredients used in pet food is the Food and Drug Administration/Center for Veterinary Medicine (FDA/CVM). Its role pertains to the labeling of the product and any health claims made by the company; for example if the food contains an ingredient(s) that prevents a particular ailment or disease.

Where Is Truth in Advertising?
Pet food advertising shows prime cuts of beef, plump chickens, whole grains, and fresh vegetables. Pet food manufacturers

want us to believe that these are the healthy wholesome ingredients used in their products. This has been very bothersome to me, and I have often questioned where is the "truth" in advertising?

I approached the Federal Trade Commission (FTC) in the United States, and Industry Canada requesting that they investigate the advertising undertaken by pet food companies. I have also requested that the labeling of these pet foods show the exact ingredients contained in the product, including road kill, condemned material from slaughterhouses, and euthanized dogs and cats.

Both government bodies have basically advised me that the pet food industry is self-regulated and therefore they have no input. In March 1999, the FTC issued a notice to rescind the Guides for the Dog and Cat Food Industry, which had empowered this organization to guard against false advertising by pet food companies. In October 1999, the FTC announced that Section 241 had been rescinded. Among other things, Section 241 covers "misleading dog or cat food in any material respect. Misrepresenting that dog and cat food is fit for human consumption. Making false statements about the conduct or the quality of a competitor's product. Using deceptive endorsements or testimonials, or deceptively claiming that any dog or cat food has received an award."

The FTC felt that the FDA's regulations and AAFCO's Model Regulations adequately covered every area of misleading advertising and labeling that are contained in Section 241 of the FTC Act. The FTC determined that its guidelines were redundant. In essence, the FTC decided to let the fox guard the chicken coop.

Industry Canada oversees the labeling and advertising of pet food. Nothing takes into account how the product ingredients can be shown or advertised. Industry Canada has basically taken the same stand as the FTC in the United States.

From 1991 until 1995 much of my time was spent meeting with Canadian government officials in an attempt to have this industry regulated. My efforts were to no avail because 95 percent of the pet food sold in Canada is imported from the United

States. Also, in Canada no government agency is involved in any aspect of the ingredients used in pet foods.

Truthful labeling must be initiated in the United States where there are some government regulations over the pet food industry. Consumers in the United States will have to push their state representatives for laws that will regulate what we feed our pets. To find out the name, address, phone number, and email address of your representative go to www.house.gov/writerep/.

Canadian consumers who are buying pet foods produced in the United States can also pressure pet food companies, or stop buying the product if they are not satisfied with the manufacturer's responses to their questions.

Both North American governments are lax in their implementation of effective regulations in the pet food industry. As one government official stated when I met with him, "The only way we will see this industry [pet food] regulated is if we [humans] start eating dogs and cats." In other words, until humans start eating cats and dogs, most likely pet food will not be strictly regulated.

Public Outcry

Pet owners are horrified to learn that rendered cats and dogs can be legally recycled back into pet food. At times, this outrage leads consumers to seek change. One case in point is Valley Protein, a rendering company that operates in twenty-two states in the Mid-Atlantic, Southeast, and Southwest regions of the United States. In the first edition of *Food Pets Die For,* I wrote about the *Baltimore City Paper* reporter Van Smith who described what he observed at the Valley Protein Rendering Plant in 1995. His article was replete with photos of barrels of dead dogs and cats about to be rendered. Smith reported that there are "thousands of dead dogs, cats, raccoons, possums, deer, foxes, snakes, and the rest that local animal shelters and roadkill patrols must dispose of each month." In that same article, Smith observed, "In a gruesomely ironic twist, most inedible dead animal parts, including dead pets, end up in feed used to fatten future generations of their kind."[1]

In March 2000, public outcry finally led to Valley Protein in Baltimore, Maryland, and Winchester, Virginia to discontinue their service of rendering euthanized domestic animals from veterinary clinics, humane societies, and animal shelters. Valley Protein issued a statement explaining, "Such services have generated much negative publicity for our organization and caused increasing concern to our valued customers."[2] Pet food companies are among their valued customers, and pet food companies in the area did not want their product to be associated with the rendering of pet carcasses.

In a May 2000 editorial, the *Warren Sentinel,* which is distributed in Warren County, Virginia, expressed concern over what would happen to the euthanized pets from shelters now that Valley Protein no longer accepts these animals. "Valley Protein has picked up euthanized animals from our shelter, and from hundreds of shelters across the eastern part of the United States for 50 years," wrote an irate employee from the Julie Wagner Animal Shelter in Warren County.[3] There were few alternatives for disposal of the shelter animals. A crematorium costs at least $30,000 and taxpayers would have to foot the bill for propane gas to fire the incinerator. The other alternative was to dump the bodies at the county landfill. This alternative would mean additional costs, including a truck and driver to transport the pet carcasses. As of May 2002, the dead animals were being taken to landfill sites, but discussions to build an incinerator were in the works.

In June 2001 another rendering plant, which had rendered pets for a number of years, refused to accept euthanized pets any longer. According to *The Times of Louisiana,* "The rendering operation cited a need to use mostly hairless farm animals for processing, which culls animal extracts for dog food, make-up and other products."[4] This rendering plant processed more than three hundred euthanized dogs and cats from the Caddo Animal Control every week. Caddo Parish is an area that covers Shreveport and Bossier City, Louisiana. Since the rendering plant stopped accepting companion animals the animal control officers at Caddo Animal Control have been trucking the carcasses to a solid waste plant where they are charged $4 per animal. A solid waste plant does not render the animals but disposes of them the way household garbage would be disposed of—either by incineration or dumpsites. The total cost for this method of disposal amounts to more then $24,000 by the end of the year. The rendering contract had cost $5,200.

The *Gainesville Sun* in Gainesville, Florida, ran a story in January 2000 on the Alachua County Animal Shelter where the employees actually had to deliver the euthanized animals to the rendering plant. According to the reporter, Paula Rausch, the employees had to "lift them off the truck and heave them into a pit exposing themselves to foul odors, putrid substances underfoot, and having to see the grinding go on."[5] These duties were taking their toll on the staff at the shelter. Shortly after the story ran, I contacted Elmira Warren, director at the shelter and she advised me that the Alachua County Animal Shelter disposed of approximately ten thousand animals annually through rendering. At that point in time the rendering plant wanted to terminate their contract with the shelter due to "bad press." As a result, the Alachua County Animal Shelter tried to secure the use of several landfill sites in the area but their request was refused. They were moving forward with plans to purchase an incinerator to dispose of the animal remains.[6]

In January 2002 I again contacted the shelter and was advised by Randy Caligiuri, operations manager, that "through a long and tedious process, we do have our own crematorium at our facility."[7] I was very pleased to hear about this small victory. That means there are at least ten thousand less animals being rendered into pet food. In addition, cremation is a lot more respectful to animal companions than dumping them in a landfill or a vat at a rendering plant.

In November 2001, Jamie Allman from KMOV-TV in St. Louis, Missouri began investigating rendering practices in St. Louis. His five-part series followed a city refuse truck, which had picked up the bodies of euthanized animals from animal shelters and delivered them to a rendering plant just across the stateline to Millstadt Rendering in Millstadt, Illinois. When Allman inquired where this material would eventually end up, a rendering plant representative asked him to leave the premises. A short time later, Allman observed a tanker truck from a southern Missouri company pull up to the plant to pick up its load. He observed that the mission of this truck was spelled out very clearly on the side of the vehicle, "Serving the pet food industry."

In December 2001, Allman reported, "The mayor of St. Louis says trucks will not be taking euthanized pets to a metro east rendering plant any more." He also reported, "St. Louis Mayor Francis Slay says Millstadt never even told the city its dead animals were winding up in pet food."[8] In the course of Allman's investigation of St. Louis rendering, he noted that pet food companies would not admit that they were getting their ingredients from Millstadt and there was no law that required that pet food companies release this information.

Because of the bad publicity, Millstadt stopped accepting euthanized pets at its facility. Dead animals from shelters in Madison County, Illinois, began to pile up in freezers. Millstadt had accepted euthanized dogs and cats from the St. Louis area for more then thirty years and now the various shelters were scrambling to find an alternative means of disposal. William Lamb from the *St. Louis Post-Dispatch* wrote, "The alternatives include building an incinerator, burying the animals in landfills or hauling them to another incinerator or rendering plant at a cost to taxpayers of tens of thousands of dollars next year."[9] Millstadt is not the only rendering plant in the area. At least two more are located in close proximity to this plant but as of this writing I have not been able to ascertain if these other plants accept dogs and cats for rendering.

Individuals Can Make a Difference

One person, on his or her own, is not going to make a drastic difference stopping renderers from accepting pets—although there are exceptions. For example, Donna English and her husband John, from Port Townsend, Washington are two consumers who made a significant difference.

After reading *Food Pets Die For,* Donna became aware that many of the shelters and veterinary clinics in Washington and Oregon were sending the euthanized animals to a rendering plant on the outskirts of Seattle, Washington. Donna and John worked tirelessly for more than two years to put together a feasibility study that proved a cremation facility would not only be self-supporting but also offer a service—cremation—that was not available in their area. In 2000 their dream reached fruition. The Jefferson County Board of Commissioners was presented with the study and eventually put the cost of the facility in the county's budget. Shelters and veterinary clinics now have a proper and dignified means of disposal for these animals. People no longer are concerned that their much loved pets might end up in pet food.

It will take hundreds of thousands of concerned pet owners putting pressure on government and pet food manufacturers before we see changes. There is strength in numbers. Circulate petitions and send them to your representatives. You can also submit a citizens' petition on behalf of your group to the FDA/CVM, requesting a ban on the use of diseased, condemned, or contaminated material in commercial pet foods.

IN THE UNITED STATES:
Federal Drug Administration
Director, Center for Veterinary Medicine
HF-1, 5600 Fishers Lane
Rockville, MD 20857

IN CANADA:
Minister of Agriculture
Ottawa, Ontario
Canada K1A OC5

It is frustrating, but don't give up. Pet owners can initiate change. One small step is better than sitting back and doing nothing. Historically, groups boycotting a particular food—taking their consumer dollars elsewhere—has worked wonders.

I have been chipping away at the pet food industry for over a decade now, and I can see that with growing consumer awareness, change is happening for the better.

The Power of the Media

It is no accident that in the United States the media are called "watch dogs." The media's job is to alert the citizenry when there is wrongdoing or controversy. The media also pay attention to consumer action. Consider contacting the media in your area if you suspect cats and dogs are being trucked to rendering plants.

If you want to get active in your community around the issue of pet food and animal companions, first, find out what is happening to the pets who are euthanized at your local shelter. Are they being cremated, buried at landfill sites, or are they sent to rendering plants? Often shelter employees are unsure of what is happening to the animals other then "a company picks them up." Find out the name of that company and contact its representatives. If the company refuses to divulge this information, contact the media, preferably an investigative reporter or team at newspapers, television stations, and radio. Express your concerns and suggest that this might be a viable story for them to cover.

If you would like to join a group concerned with the health and welfare of animals, I have listed some of the groups that have fought numerous battles for animal companions along many avenues. (See Resources.) In the United States many groups exist in every state. No doubt they would welcome someone to work in the area of pet food investigation and organization.

Change takes time and effort. If you are going to continue to feed commercial food to your companion animals, there must be change. Only through the efforts of consumers will these changes come about. Our animal companions deserve it.

RESOURCES

SUGGESTED READING MATERIAL

Anderson, N. Peiper H., DVM, *Are You Poisoning Your Pet?* East Canaan, Connecticut: Safe Goods, 1995.

Anderson, N., Peiper, H., DVM, *Super-Nutrition for Dogs n' Cats,* East Canaan, Connecticut: Safe Goods, 2000.

Belfield, W., DVM, Zucker, M., *How to Have a Healthier Dog,* New York, New York: Doubleday & Co., Inc., 1981.

Congalton, D., Alexander, C., *When Your Pet Outlives You,* Troutdale, Oregon: NewSage Press, 2002.

Cusick, W.D., *Canine Nutrition,* Wilsonville, Oregon: Doral Publishing Inc., 1997.

Derrico, K., *Unforgettable Mutts: Pure of Heart Not of Breed,* Troutdale, Oregon: NewSage Press, 1999.

Downing, R., DVM, *Pets Living with Cancer,* Lakewood, Colorado: American Animal Hospital Association Press, 2000.

Eisnitz, G.A., *Slaughterhouse,* Amherst, New York: Prometheus Books, 1997.

Fox, M.W., DVM, *Eating with Conscience: The Bioethics of Food,* Troutdale, Oregon: NewSage Press, 1997.

Fox, M.W., DVM, *Bring Life to Ethics; Global Bioethics for a Humane Society,* New York, New York: State University of New York Press, 2001.

Goldstein, M., DVM, *The Nature of Animal Healing,* New York, New York: Alfred A. Knopf, 1999.

Houston, L., *Nobody's Best Friend,* Chester, New Jersey: MCE Press, 1998.

Merwick, K., *People Food for Dogs,* Seattle, Washington: Elfin Cove Press, 1997.

Messonnier, S., DVM, *The Allergy Solution for Dogs: Natural and Conventional Therapies to Ease Discomfort and Enhance Your Dog's Quality of Life,* Roseville, California: Prima Publishing, 2000.

Messonnier, S., DVM, *Natural Health Bible for Dogs & Cats: Your A-Z Guide to Over 200 Conditions, Herbs, Vitamins, and Supplements,* Roseville, California: Prima Publishing, 2001.

Schlosser, E., *Fast Food Nation: The Dark Side of the American Meal,* New York, New York: Houghton Mifflin, 2001.

Straw, D., *Why Is Cancer Killing Our Pets?* Rochester, Vermont: Healing Arts Press, 2000.

Strombeck, D.R., DVM, *Home Prepared Dog and Cat Diets,* Ames, Iowa: Iowa State University Press, 1999.

Zucker, M., *Natural Remedies for Cats,* New York, New York: Three Rivers Press, 1999.

Zucker, M. *Natural Remedies for Dogs,* New York, New York: Three Rivers Press, 1999.

WEBSITES
IN THE UNITED STATES

American Board of Veterinary Toxicology. Provides addresses and various links to toxicology sites: **www.abvt.org**

Animal Protection Institute. An organization that informs, educates, and advocates the humane treatment of all animals: **www.api4animals/org/**

Katie Merwick. The Second Chance Ranch, provides insight into adopting, training, and nutritious feeding of animals: **www.mybluedog.com**

In Defense of Animals. This site addresses cruelty to animals and what this organization is doing to end such treatment: **www.idausa.org/index.shtml**

Wendell Belfield, DVM. Site provides information on the treatment of various pet illnesses: **www.belfield.com**

Shawn Messonnier, DVM. Visit this site to learn about natural treatments for your pets: **www.petcarenaturally.com/hospital.php**

Animal People. This is an on-line newspaper that is devoted to animal protection worldwide: **www.animalpeoplenews.org/**

Uncaged Campaigns. Located in the United Kingdom, this organization is against all animal experimentation and vivisection: **www.uncaged.co.uk/**

PubMed Medline. A database providing various case references to both human and pet diseases: **www.ncbi.nlm.nih.gov/entrez/query.fcgi**

Pet Diets. This site lists various diets for dogs, cats, and birds. Premium foods, holistic foods, and homemade diets are all discussed: **www.pets-diet.com/**

Bovine Spongiform Encephalopathy (BSE) Inquiry. This site contains the full text of the BSE Inquiry: **www.bse.org.uk/**

DogPak Rescue. Jill Richardson, DVM, provides tips to have a poison-safe household. Other information on this site includes housetraining and ending puppy mills: **www.cybrtyme.com/personal/dogpak/tips.html**

Farm Sanctuary. This organization is devoted to ending the suffering of farm animals: **www.factoryfarming.com/gallery/photos_downer.htm**

William Cusick. An outline of the regulations, or lack of, in the commercial pet food industry: **http://home.att.net/~wdcusick/03.html**

Doggie Connection Recipe Page. Many recipes, all homemade and nutritious: **www.doggieconnection.com/recipe/**

The Original Holistic Cat. This website contains a number of recipes for your feline: **www.holisticat.com/misc_recipes.html**

People for the Ethical Treatment of Animals (PETA). Promotes humane treatment of all animals including wildlife: **www.peta.org/**

Action for Animals Network. A grassroots animal rights organization located in Northern Virginia: **www.actionforanimalsnetwork.org/**

Earth Heart Foundation. This organization is dedicated to nurturing a peaceful planet: **www.uwosh.edu/organizations/alag/EarthHeart.htm#-FoundationMission**

USDA Nutrient Data Laboratory. Provides extensive data on the various vitamins, minerals, and amino acids in foods: **www.nal.usda.gov/fnic/foodcomp/**

IN CANADA

Animal Alliance of Canada. This organization is dedicated to the protection of all animals and to promote a harmonious relationship among people, animals, and the environment: **www.animalalliance.ca/**

Vancouver Humane Society. Promotes animal protection through education and advocacy: **www.vancouverhumanesociety.bc.ca/home.html**

The Kindness Club. The Kindness Club is a humane and environmental education organization for children: **www.smythe.nbcc.nb.ca/kindness/**

Voice for the Voiceless. A Vancouver-based organization devoted to education and awareness of animals in need of assistance: **www.clix.to/v4v1**

IN THE UNITED KINGDOM

Animal Aid. This is the largest animals rights organization in the United Kingdom and one of the oldest in the world: **www.animalaid.org.uk/**

Animal Defenders. The purpose of the Animal Defenders is to educate, create awareness, and promote the interest of humanity in the cause of justice, and the suppression of all forms of cruelty to animals: **www.animaldefenders.org.uk/**

The Humane Research Trust. The first trust to promote medical and scientific research replacing the use of animals: **www.btinternet.com/~shawweb/hrt/index.htm**

ENDNOTES

CHAPTER ONE:
What Goes Into Commercial Pet Foods

1. David C. Cooke, "Euthanasia of the Companion Animal," Animal Disposal: Fact or Fiction," American Veterinarians Medical Association, Panel on Euthanasia, 1988, p. 227.

2. H. Winter Griffith, *Complete Guide to Vitamins, Minerals and Other Supplements,* Tucson, Arizona: Fisher Books, 1988, p. 49.

3. Extoxnet Extension Toxicology Network, "Breakdown of Chemicals in Vegetation," Cornell University, Michigan State University, Oregon State University and University of California at Davis, Paper, May 1994.

4. Wendell Belfield, DVM, to Sharon Benz, Center for Veterinary Medicine, letter, March 25, 2002.

5. The Animal Protection Institute, Investigative Report, May 1996.

6. United States Department of Agriculture, Food Inspection Services, "Condemned and Inedible Products," Regulation 18.1, January 2001.

7. Personal correspondence with AAFCO, the Department of Agriculture, State of Delaware, September 23, 1994.

CHAPTER TWO
Companion Animals In Pet Food
1. Personal correspondence with Alan Schulman, DVM, Los Angeles, California, July 24, 2000.

2. John Eckhouse, "How Dogs and Cats Get Recycled Into Pet Food," *San Francisco Chronicle,* February 19, 1990.

3. Personal correspondence with Phil Morgan, Escondido Humane Society, Escondido, California, July 28, 2000.

4. Personal correspondence with Christine Richmond, Division of Animal Feed, Food and Drug Administration, Center for Veterinary Medicine, (FDA/CVM) June 24, 1994.

5. Sandra Blakeslee, "Disease Fear Prompts New Look at Rendering," *The New York Times,* March 11, 1997.

6. Ibid.

7. Environmental Protection Act. Section 9.5.3 "Meat Rendering Plants." http://www.epa.gov/ttn/chief/ap42/ch09/final/c9s05-3.pdf

8. Personal correspondence with Government du Quebec, Department of Food, Fisheries, and Agriculture, August 14, 1992.

9. Personal correspondence with Tom Baker, Ontario Ministry of Agriculture and Food, June 13, 2001.

10. Colin Freeze, "Animal Feed to Exclude Cat, Dogs," *Globe and Mail,* June 4, 2001.

11. Philip Lee-Shanok "Is Your Animal a Cannibal?" *Toronto Sun,* June 7, 2001.

12. Personal correspondence with Isabelle Trudeau, Ministry of Agriculture, Quebec, June 6, 2001.

13. Food and Drug Administration, Center for Veterinary Medicine, "Food and Drug Administration/Center for Veterinary Medicine. Report on the risk from pentobarbital in dog food," March 28, 2002. www.fda/gov/cvm/efoi/efoi/html

14. Peter Faletra, PhD, "DNA and Heat," Office of Science, Department of Energy, University of Chicago, Molecular Biology, 2000. http://newton.dep.anl.gov/askasci/mole00/mole00136.htm

15. Personal correspondence with Albert Harper, PhD, Director of The Henry C. Lee Institute of Forensic Science, University of New Haven. July 17, 2002.

16. Personal correspondence with Rainer Schubbert, DVM, MediGenomix, Martinsried, Germany, March 13, 2002.

17. Personal correspondence with R.A. Bowen, Department of Biomedical Science, Colorado State University, Fort Collins, Colorado, March 2, 2002.

18. Personal correspondence with Gene Weddington, PhD, May 24, 2001.

CHAPTER THREE
Sodium Pentobarbital in Pet Food

1. Personal correspondence with Lori L. Miser, DVM, Illinois Department of Agriculture, Bureau of Animal Health, March 11, 2002.

2. "2000 Report of the American Veterinary Medical Association Panel on Euthanasia, *Journal of the American Veterinary Medical Association,* Vol. 218, No. 5, March 1, 2001, p. 685.

3. Ibid.

4. John J. O'Connor, DVM, MPH; Clarence M. Stowe, VMD, PhD; Robert R. Robinson, BVSc, MPH, PhD, "Fate of Sodium Pentobarbital in Rendered Material, " *American Journal of Veterinary Research,* Vol. 46, No. 8, August 1995, pp. 1721, 1723.

5. United States Animal Health Association, "Report of the USAHA Committee on Feed Safety," 1998 Committee Report, October 7, 1998.

6. Personal correspondence with Wanda Russ, Policy Analyst, FDA, Executive Secretariat, February 8, 2001.

7. Personal correspondence with Marilyn Broderick, Consumer Safety Office, Office of Management and Communication, Center for Veterinary Medicine, September 13, 2001.

8. Ibid.

9. Ibid.

10. Food and Drug Administration, Center for Veterinary Medicine, "Food and Drug Administration/Center for Veterinary Medicine, Report on the risk from pentobarbital in dog food," March 28, 2002. www.fda/gov/cvm/efoi/efoi/html

11. Ibid.

12. Ibid.

13. Ibid.

14. Animal Ark, "Study Finds Euthanasia Agent in Pet Foods," Report, March 30, 2002.

15. Personal correspondence with Linda Grassie, Public Information Specialist, FDA/Center for Veterinary Medicine, March 17, 2002.

16. Ibid.

17. Personal correspondence with Wayne E. Cunningham, DVM, MS, Colorado State Veterinarian, March 1, 2002.

18. Personal correspondence with Leroy Coffman, DVM, Florida State Veterinarian, March 4, 2002.

19. Personal correspondence with Wayne Flory, Texas Veterinary Medical Diagnostic Laboratory, Texas A&M University, March 4, 2002.

20. Personal correspondence with Helene Chagnon, DVM, Agriculture Canada, Veterinary Products Consultant, March 18, 2002.

21. Lori L. Miser, op. cit.

22. California Department of Food and Agriculture, Animal Health and Food Safety Services, Animal Care Program, "The Emergency Euthanasia of Horses," Information Sheet, November 1999.

23. Kate O'Rourke, American Veterinary Medical Association, "Euthanized animals can poison wildlife: Veterinarians receive fine," Report, January 15, 2002.

24. Ibid.

25. National Euthanasia Registry, http://www.usner.org/press.htm

26. Ibid.

CHAPTER FOUR:
Pet Food Regulations

1. Sharon Benz, PhD, FDA's Regulation of Pet Food, "Information for Consumers," 2001.

2. Personal correspondence with Linda Grassie, Food and Drug Administration, Center for Veterinary Medicine, January 7, 2002.

3. Department of Agriculture, "Association of American Feed Control Officials Feed Check Sample Program," State of Colorado, Information Sheet, 2001.

4. Ibid.

5. Personal correspondence with Nancy Cook, VP of Technical and Regulatory Affairs, Pet Food Institute, April 28, 2000.

6. Pet Food Institute, "A Consumers Guide to Pet Foods," Report, September 2002.

7. Personal correspondence with Denise Spencer, DVM, Senior Staff Veterinarian, United States Department of Agriculture, National Center for Import and Export, January 8, 2002.

8. Government of Canada, Canadian Food Inspection Agency, "Animal Health and Production Division: Import Procedures," Regulations, April 6, 2001.

9. European Economic Council, "Guidelines for pet food exports to Europe," Council Directive 90/667/Eurasian Economic Community (EEC), April 1997.

10. The Pet Food Manufacturer's Association, U.K., 2001. www.pfma.com/about.htm

11. Personal correspondence with Alison Walker, spokesperson for the Pet Food Manufacturers Association, UK, March 19, 2002.

12. *The Japanese Market News,* "Pet Food," 2001. www.wtcjapan.ne.jp/jmn/petfood.html

CHAPTER FIVE
Pet Food Manufacturers
1. Euromonitor International, "Pet Foods and Accessories in the USA, Report, October 2001.

2. Institute of Food Science and Engineering, "Kal Kan Pet Care," Texas A&M University, Paper, 2001.

3. Hannah Cowdy, "Royal Canin pet food buy makes Mars Europe top dog," Reuters, July 10, 2001.

4. Good Dog News Service, "Iams to Be Sold Everywhere," January 15, 2000. www.gooddogmagazine.com

5. KMOV-TV, St. Louis Missouri, "FTC approves Nestlé's $10.3 billion purchase of Ralston Purina," Report, December 11, 2001.

6. Federal Trade Commission, "Analysis of Proposed Consent Order to Aid Public Comment," December 11, 2001.

7. Julie Thompson, "Pet Food Giant Target of Rivals' Lawsuit," *Dayton Business Journal,* March 16, 2001.

8. Greg Johnson, "Clawing to Become Top Dog of Pet Food," *Los Angeles Times,* October 22, 2001.

9. Wasserman, Comden & Casselman, L.L.P. "Class Action Against the Iams Company," Paper, March 5, 2001.

10. Ibid.

11. The Bureau of National Affairs Inc., Class Action Litigation, Class Action Filings, Vol. 02, No. 06, ISSN 1529-8000, March 23, 2001, p. 192.

12. College of Veterinary Medicine and Biomedical Sciences, Executive Council Minutes, June 8, 2000.

13. Ralston Purina, "Ralston Purina Funds Three New Veterinary Diet Technician Positions," Press release, May 10, 2000.

14. The American Veterinary Medical Association, "Bayer, Hill's Make a Commitment...Not Seen Before," Press release, September 15, 1997.

15. The Humane Society of the United States, "Hill's Science Diet Signed as Major Sponsor of HSUS Programs." Companion Animal Update, Newsletter, February 2002.

16. Ibid.

17. Ralston Purina, "Ralston Purina Donations Benefit the AKC Canine Health Foundation, Press release, February 27, 1999.

CHAPTER SIX
Mad Cow Disease and Pet Food
1. Stanley B. Prusiner, MD, "The Prion Diseases," *Scientific American,* January 1995, p. 50.

2. The BSE Inquiry: The Report, "Industry Process and Controls: Rendering, Vol. 13, Section 6.48, 2000.

3. Steven Best, Associate Professor of Philosophy and Humanities, "Cows, Cannibalism, Capitalism & Coverup: The Politics and Economics of Mad Cow Disease," Paper, 1999.

4. Boller, Francois, et al, "Diagnosis of Dementia: Clinicopathological Correlations," *Neurology,* January 1989, pp. 76-79.

5. Manuelidis, E.E., et al, Suggested Links Between Different Types of Dementias: "Creutzfeld-Jakob disease, Alzheimer disease and Retroviral CNS Infections," Alzheimer Disease and Associated Disorders, Vol 3, No. 1-2, 1989, pp. 100-109.

6. Lukas Perler, The Federal Veterinary Office, "Spongiform Encephalopathy in a Cat," Press release, Bern, July 17, 2001.

7. Neuro Center, Reference Laboratory for Spongiform Encephalophies in Animals. www.neurocenter-bern.ch/tse_e.shtml#box2

8. Species, August 31, 2002, www.defra.gov Department of Environment, Food, Rural Affairs (DEFRA). Exoctic.uk/animalh/bse/-bse-statistics/level-3-tsestat.html#ref_10

9. Gardner Murray, Chief Veterinary Officer, Department of Agriculture, Fisheries and Forestry Australia, (AFFA), Canberra, Report, July 29, 2002.

10. United States Department of Agriculture, Animal and Plant Health Inspection Services, "Scrapie," Bulletin, August 2001.

11. *The New York Times*, "Mad Cow May have been caused by animal rendering plants," March 11, 1997.

12. The BSE Inquiry, "Comparison of UK rendering process in other countries," Vol. 13: Processes and Controls, Annex C to Chapter 6: 6.99, 2000.

13. Joel McNair, "BSE: A Ticking Time Bomb in Downer Cows?" *Agri-View*, June 17, 1993.

14. Statement by anonymous United States Department of Agriculture employee e-mail, January 11, 1997.

15. Western Association of Fish and Wildlife Agencies and the Western Wildlife Health Cooperative "Chronic Wasting Disease in Big Game Mammals," Newsletter, 2001.

16. Personal correspondence with Beth Williams, DVM, Department of Veterinary Services, University of Wyoming, March 18, 2001.

17. United States Department of Agriculture-Animal and Plant Health Inspection Service, "What Types of BSE Surveillance are We Doing," Information Sheet, 2002.

18. Public Citizen, "Study Finds Flaws in 'Mad Cow' Detection Program," Report, July 19, 2001.

19. Food Animal Concern Trust (FACT), "Prevention of Mad Cow Disease in America," Information Sheet, April 2001.

20. Steve Stecklow, "The US May Face Mad-Cow Exposure Despite Assurances from Government," *Wall Street Journal*, November 28, 2001.

21. Steven Best, op.cit.

22. Jeffery A. Nelson, "USDA Mad Cow Strategy: Don't Look, Don't Find," *VegSource*, Article, http://www.vegsource.com April 2, 2001.

23. Personal correspondence with Arthur J. Davis, National Veterinary Laboratory Services, Ames, Iowa, March 27, 2000.

24. Jeffery Nelson, op.cit.

25. Personal correspondence with Peter Mueller, Prionics AG, Schlieren, Switzerland, September 16, 2002.

26. Jeffery A. Nelson, opt. cit.

27. Associated Press, "FDA: U.S. feed mills breaking mad cow rules," March 23, 2001.

28. Chip Chandler, "Witness testifies some ill cattle sent to rendering plant," *Amarillo Globe-News*, January 23, 1998.

29. Michael S. Marquis, Assistant Director, Executive Correspondence and Freedom of Information Act, United States Department of Agriculture, January 29, 2002.

30. Personal correspondence with Scott McEwen, DVM, Veterinary College, University of Guelph, Ontario, October 21, 1996.

31. Julie Ingwersen, "Pet Food Makers Have No Plans To Stop Using Meat and Bone Meal," Reuters, March 24, 2001.

CHAPTER SEVEN
Pet Food Companies and Animal Experiments

1. The Center for Laboratory Animal Welfare, "Product Testing," 2002. www.-labanimalwelfare.org/product_testing.html

2. Nancy L. Harrison, MD, Doctors Against Dog Labs, Report, August 15, 2002.

3. The Humane Society of the United States, "Controversial OSU Researcher Will Depart This Summer," Report, June 14, 2002.

4. Lucy Johnston, Health Editor, "Iams-Pet Food Cruelty Exposed," *Sunday Express*, May 27, 2001.

5. Uncaged Campaigns, "Iams—The Suffering Behind the Science," June 1, 2001. www.uncaged.co.uk/iams.htm

6. Animal People Online, "Pet Food and Procter and Gamble," June 2001. http://207.36.38.241/01/6/petfoodAP0601.html

7. Uncaged Campaigns, op.cit.

8. Katherine Stitzel, P&G Associated Director, interview in UK with Animal People, June 26, 2001.

9. Lawrence Carter-Long, "Stop Torturing Animals for Pet Food Research," Animal Protection Institute, Press release, August 6, 2001.

10. British Union for the Abolition of Vivisection, "In The Can-Pet Food Tests Expose," Press release, June 2000.

11. Ibid.

12. Ibid.

13. Ibid.

14. Ibid.

15. Paula Kislak, DVM, Association of Veterinarians for Animal Rights, in reply to query from Danielle Marino, September 28, 2001.

16. Uncaged Campaigns, op.cit.,

17. In Defense of Animals, "Iams Award Pays Tribute to Cruel Scientist," News release, January 4, 2002.

CHAPTER EIGHT
Homecooked Meals
and All Natural Pet Food Companies
1. Wendell Belfield and Martin Zucker, *How to Have a Healthier Dog*, New York: Doubleday and Company, 1981, p. 42.

2. Pat Lazarus, *Keep Your Pet Healthy the Natural Way*, New Canaan, Connecticut: Keats Publishing, 1993, pp. 21-37.

3. Martin Goldstein, DVM, *The Nature of Animal Healing*, New York, New York: Ballantine Books, 1999, p. 127.

4. Martin Zucker, Natural *Remedies for Dogs*, New York, New York: Three Rivers Press, 1999, p. 44.

5. Martin Zucker, Natural *Remedies for Cats*, New York, New York: Three Rivers Press, 1999, p. 49.

6. Riveriene Farm, Nutrition Index www3.-sk.simpatico.ca/riverien/nutridglike.htm

7. Wendell Belfield and Martin Zucker, *How to Have a Healthier Dog*, New York, New York: Doubleday and Company, 1981, p. 89.

8. Anitra Fraser with Norma Eckrote, *The New Natural Cat*, New York, New York: Dutton, 1990, p. 52.

9. Richard Pitcairn, *Dr. Pitcairn's Complete Guide to Natural Health for Dogs and Cats*, Emmaus, Pennsylvania: Rodale Press, Inc., 1982, p. 19.

10. Shawn Messonnier, DVM, "Proper Nutrition Makes for a Healthier Pet," *Natural Horse Magazine*, Vol. 1, Issue 7, 1999.

CHAPTER NINE:
Vitamins and Supplements
1. Martin Goldstein, DVM, *The Nature of Animal Healing*, New York, New York: Ballantine Books, 1999, p. 127.

2. Deborah Straw, *Why Is Cancer Killing Our Pets,?* Rochester, Vermont: Healing Arts Press, 2000, p. 138.

3. Shawn Messonnier, *Natural Health Bible for Dogs & Cats:* Roseville, California: Prima Publishing, 2001, p. 5.

4. Nancy Scanlan, DVM, "Pets Need Supplements, Too," Atma Center Online, Fall 1998. www.atmacenter.com/fall98/pets.html

CHAPTER ELEVEN
Other Toxic Products
1. National Animal Poison Control Center, "Plants Poisonous to Dogs and Cats," 2002.

2. Howard M. Hayes, Robert E. Tarone, Kenneth P. Cantor, Carl R. Jennsen, Denis McCurrin, Ralph C. Richardson, "2,4-Dichlorphenoxyacetic Acid," *Journal of the National Cancer Institute*, Vol. 83, No. 17, September 4, 1991.

3. Ibid.

4. Fraser Hale, DVM, FAVD, Dipl. AVDC, Guelph, Ontario, personal correspondence, October 11, 2000.

5. Jeff Gordon, "It's Not Epilepsy. It's MSG," Paper, March 6, 1998.

6. Gail Davis, *The Complete Guide to Vegetarian Convenience Foods,* Troutdale, Oregon: NewSage Press, 1999, p. 131.

7. Ibid.

8. The Pet Consumer Report, "Kitty Litter with a Serious Warning," www.petconsumer-report.com 2002.

CHAPTER TWELVE
Consumer Action
1. Van Smith, "Meltdown," *City Paper,* Baltimore, Maryland, September 27, 1995.

2. Bridgette Blair, Dan Reany. "Valley Protein Inc. Will End Euthanized Animal Service," *The Winchester Star,* March 8, 2000.

3. "Get Outraged," *The Warren Sentinel,* 'Opinion Page,' Warren County, Virginia, March 9, 2000.

4. *The Times of Louisiana,* June 21, 2001.

5. Paula Rausch, "County Seeks Pet Disposal Alternative," *The Gainesville Sun,* January 5, 2000.

6. Personal correspondence with Elmira Warren, Alachua County Animal Services, September 12, 2000.

7. Personal correspondence with Randy Caligiuri, Alachua County Animal Services, January 2, 2002.

8. Jamie Allman, "Mayor: Pets from city pound will not go to plant," KMOV-TV, December 14, 2001.

9. William Lamb, "Outcry leads to changes in disposal of animals," *St. Louis Post-Dispatch,* December 19, 2001.

INDEX

ABOUT THE AUTHOR

A NN MARTIN is internationally recognized as an authority on the commercial pet food controversy. Since 1990, Martin has investigated and questioned exactly what goes into most commercial pet food and continues to discover more unsavory practices of the pet food industry.

The first edition of *Food Pets Die For: Shocking Facts About Pet Food,* published in 1997, was the first book to expose the hazards

Ann Martin and Sarge

of commercial pet food. Ms. Martin's investigative reporting was selected for special recognition as "one of the most censored news stories of 1997" by Sonoma State University's *Project Censored,* which focuses on important news events that are largely ignored by mainstream media. Since then, she has been on numerous television and radio shows, internationally and her book has been translated into Japanese. Ms. Martin is also a columnist for *Better Nutrition* magazine. In her second book, *Protect Your Pet: More Shocking Facts,* Ms. Martin continues her investigation of commercial pet food as well as other controversial, pet-related issues.

Ms. Martin graduated with a B.A. in business from the University of Western Ontario, and worked in a tax office for several years. She lives in Ontario, Canada with her animal companions, where she continues to question, research, and write about pet-related issues. She can be reached by email at anmartin1@rogers.com or you can reach her through NewSage Press's website.

www.newsagepress.com

ALSO BY ANN MARTIN

Protect Your Pet: More Shocking Facts

In her second book, *Protect Your Pet* (NewSage Press 2001), Ann Martin continues her thorough investigation of pet-related issues. She examines the popular raw meat diet; the latest information on the controversy surrounding yearly vaccinations; increased cancer in pets and over-vaccination; alternatives in vaccination protocols; and the latest on the controversy of using Rimadyl for arthritic dogs. The final chapter offers more healthy homemade recipes for cats and dogs.

Praise for Protect Your Pet

The pet food industry and its allies dictate thinking for pet owners and veterinarians on feeding pets. *Protect Your Pet* discusses important problems the industry refuses to address. It also documents truths on other issues that veterinarians choose to ignore. This book is an essential resource that all pet owners should read.

—DONALD R. STROMBECK, DVM, PhD
Professor Emeritus, UC Davis, School of Veterinary Medicine
Author, *Home Prepared Dog and Cat Diets*

This informative book offers excellent information that will help the pet owner to determine which diets are most beneficial. Good health can only be accomplished through good nutrition.

—WENDELL BELFIELD, DVM
Author, *How to Have a Healthier Dog*

In *Food Pets Die For*, which has sold more than 20,000 copies, Ann N. Martin censured the pet food industry with meticulous evidence of contaminants in commercial food that can cause degenerative diseases and even death.... Though it may provoke disgust and outrage, pet owners who want the best for their cats and dogs should read this book.

—*Publishers Weekly*

OTHER TITLES BY NEWSAGE PRESS

NewSage Press has published several titles related to animals. We hope these books will inspire humanity towards a more compassionate and respectful treatment of all living beings.

Protect Your Pet: More Shocking Facts
  by Ann N. Martin

Pets at Risk: From Allergies to Cancer, Remedies for an
  Unsuspected Epidemic
  by Alfred J. Plechner, D.V.M. with Martin Zucker

When Your Pet Outlives You:
  Protecting Animal Companions After You Die
  by David Congalton & Charlotte Alexander
  Award Winner, CWA Muse Medallion 2002

Blessing the Bridge:
  What Animals Teach Us About Death, Dying, and Beyond
  by Rita M. Reynolds

Three Cats, Two Dogs, One Journey Through Multiple Pet Loss
  by David Congalton
  Award Winner, Merial Human-Animal Bond, Best Book

Conversations with Animals: Cherished Messages and Memories
  as Told by an Animal Communicator
  by Lydia Hiby with Bonnie Weintraub

Polar Dream: The First Solo Expedition by a Woman and
  Her Dog to the Magnetic North Pole
  by Helen Thayer, Foreword by Sir Edmund Hillary

The Wolf, the Woman, the Wilderness:
  A True Story of Returning Home
  by Teresa Tsimmu Martino

Dancer on the Grass: True Stories About Horses and People
  by Teresa Tsimmu Martino

Unforgettable Mutts: Pure of Heart Not of Breed
  by Karen Derrico

NewSage Press
PO Box 607, Troutdale, OR 97060-0607

Phone Toll Free 877-695-2211, Fax 503-695-5406
Email: info@newsagepress.com, or www.newsagepress.com

Distributed to bookstores by Publishers Group West
800-788-3123, PGW Canada 800-463-3981